D0058329

A View From the Red Tees

A View From the Red Tees
The Truth About Women and Golf

Dorothy Langley

A Citadel Press Book
Published by Carol Publishing Group

A Citadel Press Book
Published by Carol Publishing Group
Citadel Press is a registered trademark of Carol Communications, Inc.

Editorial, sales and distribution, rights and permissions inquiries should be addressed to Carol Publishing Group, 120 Enterprise Avenue, Secaucus, N.J. 07094

In Canada: Canadian Manda Group, One Atlantic Avenue, Suite 105, Toronto, Ontario M6K 3E7

Carol Publishing Group books may be purchased in bulk at special discounts for sales promotion, fund-raising, or educational purposes. Special editions can be created to specifications. For details, contact Special Sales Department, Carol Publishing Group, 120 Enterprise Avenue, Secaucus, N.J. 07094.

Manufactured in the United States of America

10 9 8 7 6 5 4 3 2 1

Library of Congress Cataloging-in-Publication Data

Langley, Dorothy.
    A view from the red tees : the truth about women and golf / by Dorothy Langley.
        p.   cm.
    "A Citadel Press book."
    ISBN 1–55972–440–4
    1. Golf for women.   I. Title.
GV966.L36   1997   97–17002
                                                  CIP

To
all of my friends on the red tees
and
to the good guys on the white ones

Contents

The Putting Green

The Foreword Before the Fairway

A View From the Red Tees is a book about you, me, and all of the women we know who have heard and answered the call of the ball. It is a tongue-in-cheek celebration of how and why we women play golf and the joys and frustrations the sport brings us.

A View From the Red Tees examines how golf affects our relationships with each other, our families, and our colleagues. It looks at the clubs we buy, the clothes we wear, and the friends we make.

I also poke fun in this book at the men who don't want to play with us and don't want to play behind us. I laugh at the golf store salesclerk who greets the woman golfer with, "Are you looking for something for your husband today?"

You can rest assured that this book is at all times politically correct. In other words, I bashed the heck out of men anytime I could get away with it. That's because I wrote this book after I read the results of a certain study. That study indicated that about 80 percent of women golfers consider men a source of intimidation on the golf course. Just think of it. That must mean that 80 percent of the 5.4 million women who golf in the United States today are scared to death of being paired up with men golfers. Who could blame them? I feel the same way. Men play a pretty intimidating game. All those errant balls they hit. If one of those babies hit you, you really could get hurt badly.

A View From the Red Tees is meant to be more fun than funny. I wrote this book because I want women golfers to feel good. I want them to feel good about themselves, their games, and their lives. I want every one of them to take a risk once in a while and get paired up with three unknown men.

We women are, after all, members of a very special club. We're the Red Tees People.

Acknowledgments

Loving thanks to those people who have helped me with this book. I am particularly grateful to:

Bryan, for believing in me and my book and for giving me such expert computer support

Mother, for sharing with me her wonderful insights into writing

Jan and Janice, for taking me golfing the first time ever

Gretchen, for being so enthusiastic during my weekly writing-progress reports

Nancy, for always being so willing to play a good round of golf.

A View From the Red Tees

First Hole

Women Play the Game

Why Women Are Better Golfers Than Men

What is true in the game of life is also true in golf. Women play better than men.

Reason One: Women play with their clubs, not with their egos

Men do not have the positive mental approach toward golf we women do. Consider what happens when a man does not play to the handicap he has not played to since he quit his college golf team twenty years ago. He throws tantrums and clubs.

In contrast, we women are emotionally equipped for a bad day on the course. When we play poorly, we take responsibility for our game. We admit that we should have known better than to play this course when it was in this condition. We admit that we should never have played with these clubs that we need to replace. We acknowledge that we always play poorly when our shadow is in the line of every swing we take. In other words, we take responsibility. We may even joke, "Hey, I don't think a lesson or two would hurt my game *too* much."

Men who are having a bad ball day dwell on how much better they played last time. A man playing poorly hints that the reason for his poor golf is his present company. It is a casual comment. "Hey, last time I played, when, by the way, I played very, very well, I was playing with golfers of the same caliber."

Does he mean by this that everyone else was double and triple bogeying every hole, as he is now? No, not at all. He is instead implying that your bogeys and pars do not sufficiently challenge him. How the heck is he supposed to be motivated to birdie a hole when you are only bogeying yours?

Compare this behavior to the woman who is playing poorly. She does not focus on your game. She puts a plan of action together for her own, instead. She asks her golf mates if they know where she might find a good female pro. Better yet, she may ask them where they think she should sign up for one of those five-day, $2,000 golf schools that all the male colleagues in her office attend but pretend they never heard of.

Playing with a woman who is playing poorly is like playing with a woman who is playing well. In other words, it is enjoyable. There is really nothing less pleasant than playing golf with a man who is playing poorly, however. Well, unless, of course, you consider what it is like playing golf with a man who happens to be playing exceptionally well.

The first thing you will notice about a man playing at his best is that he will assure you that this is not his best at all. So what if he has a 25 handicap and he is only 7-over-par on the front nine? He is not playing out of his league today. He is not a sandbagger. No, the problem is he usually has great shots like the ones he has had today throughout his game. Just the results are different. Today he is finally making the scores he deserves. He is ready for this success.

A man golfer-in-the-zone is not content to enjoy his newfound success quietly. After all, he is now so-o-o-o good. It would be unfair not to let all the others know that they ought to be watching him. Thus, a man golfer-in-the-zone is like a comic strip mother-in-law or a neighbor's dog in heat. He barks loudly at you every time you move. He flaunts his successes for the world to see. Plus he whines incessantly the moment you stop patting his back and pay attention to your own back(swing). A man golfer-in-the-zone grooves doubts in your gray matter. He alters your swing thoughts and reverse engineers your ten-year capital investment in positive-thought management.

Let's say you are just about to begin your backswing. The sun is on your back. You are poised. The world is quiet and sweet. All of a sudden, he booms: "Hey! You're using the wrong club!" You top the ball. He smiles. "I told you so!"

Let's say you are 150 yards from the green. You have 75 yards of fairway in front of you and then a 75-yard lake to cross. You decide to go for it. You hit with your 5-wood. Your ball looks like a perfect shot until it hits a rock on the other side of the lake, takes an unlucky bounce, and splashes into the water. The man-in-the-zone yells to you, "Don't feel bad. You're doing all right. You just need to learn your limitations!"

You wonder where your confidence went when you come to the next hole. It is an 80-yard par-3 that has a 15-yard sand trap in front of the green. You decide you'd better lay up. Nodding approvingly at your club selection on this hole, the man-in-the-zone bestows just one tiny final bit of advice: "Just keep your head low, your left arm stiff, and whack the bejeebies out of that ball!" You begin to have trouble concentrating on your shot. Your curiosity begins to itch. If only you had the answer to one question. "How would Harvey Penick say you should handle a golfer like this?"

Reason Two: Women recognize the most deadly hazard on the golf course, flying balls

Women golfers do not play better than men only because they respect the mental side of the game. Unlike men, we also understand that, since golf is a sport, there are basic safety rules. Men golfers routinely hit balls into the women golfers in front of them. They consider the hostile intrusion of their balls into the women's playing area equivalent to the announcement of an emperor's proclamation: "Hey ladies! There is a male group behind you. You better speed up play!"

It makes no difference if these women are waiting for the male foursome in front of them to proceed with their play. The men do not know this. They just want to intimidate the women enough to let them pass through. If the women let them through and there is no place for them to go, one explains to the others, "Heck! We were waiting and there was a group of women in front of us. What were we supposed to think? That it wasn't their fault? Duhhhh…"

"Yeah, you're right," agrees his partner, "there is nothing personal here. Just a simple fact-finding mission. That's all that scout ball was… a simple fact-finding mission."

Just as mountain climbers will come to the aid of those who are in trouble before proceeding toward the summit, however, women golfers value the safety of other golfers more than their own speedy advancement on the course. A female foursome does not hit into a group that is holding them up.

Men golfers tell each other the reason women do not hit into them is not related to etiquette but rather to capability. "Don't worry about those ladies behind us. No way they can hit far enough to hit into us." They will also tell a woman the same thing. Well, unless, of course, she routinely happens to hit farther than they do when she is hitting from the red (or, heaven forbid, the white) tees. Then they just will say she is an exceptional golfer who does not play like other women.

When male golfers hit into other male golfers, they apologize. If they don't apologize, some member of the leading group may hit the ball back at them. Men golfers do not apologize to women for their aggressive drives, however. Why should they apologize, they reason, when the problem is that women play slow. Unlike men, women golfers do not hit the ball back. Women are concerned that the returning ball could hurt someone. It even could hurt someone who did not strike it in their vicinity initially.

A woman golfer thus will simply pick up and pocket an offending ball. She then calmly will wait five minutes after the male foursome has spent ten minutes looking for the ball. She might even be so courteous as to drive back in her golf cart and give it back.

"Lady, I wish you had told us you picked up the ball. Do you remember where it landed?" the offending golfer will say to her.

She will point to a spot fifty yards back from its original resting place, behind some tree or in a sand trap, and say, "It was right about there. Now don't hit into us again. I'm trying to take a little break from my legal practice out here!"

Reason Three: Women understand that our first shots are not the only shots that count

Women golfers play eighteen holes of golf. Men golfers drive eighteen tee shots interrupted by some short stuff.

Men love the idea of a long drive. They love it even more than they love their mulligans. This is why the only people who use 3-woods on the tee box of a par-4 hole are women golfers. The average man golfer owns the most powerful driver he can afford. Well, it may not be so powerful in his hands. In fact, the average male golfer hits his tee shots 30 yards longer and 130 yards straighter with his 3-woods than with his driver. A man, however, like many women, likes to use his driver on the tee box. He can just sort of imagine the success it would bring him if he were Tiger Woods instead of Duffer Dan.

Remember those boasts the boy next door used to make? "My dog is meaner than yours." "My dad is bigger than yours." The golfing man is too mature for that kind of nonsense. He speaks through his actions. Can't you hear him as he pulls his club out of his bag? "I have the meanest and longest club on the course."

Who are we women to laugh, though? We know calling a man's Killer Bee a bumblebee or his Great Big Bertha a great big bust would be like calling his pit bull a poodle. Them's betting words. Big betting words. We women don't like to bet that big. Moreover, whom are we kidding? We use the ladies' version of those same clubs anyway.

The quest for distance motivates every golfer, regardless of means or gender. Like men, women golfers also love to hit long drives. We love to wallop the heck out of our balls. Women are different from men, though. We actually care about the result. It is more than an advantage if our ball ends up in our fairway; it is a fulfilled expectation.

In fact, one of the reasons we women play better than men is because our games are boringly predictable. Women golfers make fewer spectacular shots over trees, from under bridges, and across fairways. We also tend to be less able to do so. Let's face it. We just get less practice than men in what I call the "extreme golf experience."

Men are different from women in other ways, too. A woman golfer always wants to whip her ball as far as possible. A man, however, will always *need* to get that baby out there. It does not matter if he slices it into the adjoining fairway, plunges it six inches deep into a sand trap, or hooks it deep into the woods. The question is, was it a good shot? In other words, did it go far? Did it go farther than everyone else's?

Thus, the two genders play different games and women play a better one. Why is that? Is it genetics? Early conditioning? What makes men, rather than women, concentrate on distance over score?

Well, realistically, the average woman golfer does not have the physique that would allow her to get as much distance from a swing as a man her height could. We may be less obsessed because we are less able. What I believe is even more important, however, is that men get more positive (albeit falsely positive) reinforcement for their shots than women get. Men are not as accurate in yardage determination as women are. They tend to think they have hit their balls farther than they actually have.

Men do not make this error deliberately. They simply use a different, less credible measure of distance than we women do. Women know how far we have hit because we use the distance markers available on the course to calculate our ball's progress toward the hole. Men, on the other hand, compare their ball distances with an enhanced-six-inch mental ruler. You know, the one with which they compared each other's nongolfing appendages as adolescents. This error alone adds about 25 percent onto their yardage.

Perhaps the major reason men emphasize distance over score, however, is that they consider distance more revealing than score. Men carefully massage—I mean, manage—their scores, unlike us women players. Men, unlike us, honor the primary sacrament of handicap integrity: they never, ever write down a score on any hole that exceeds the magical amount their handicap allows. They also practice another rule. They never add a stroke they hit within fifty yards of another one unless, of course, it is their second putt. Since distance is thus a more reliable credential for men than score, they believe the longest driver is the best golfer.

On the nineteenth hole, a man golfer can and will tell you who shot the longest drive on every hole he played that day. That is, he can and will, unless a woman was the longest driver. "A very lucky woman," he might add. In that case, he may chide you and say that such comparisons are childish.

On the nineteenth hole, a man may also point to his low score to contradict any assertion that women play better than men. Even if his luck is such that his score is lower, we must remember there is more to the game than a posted score. There is also the question as to how the game was played.

Reason Four: Women golfers practice the Zen of golf instead of the zeal of shot-making

Women are better golfers than men because they appreciate the true nature of golf. Golf is more than a sport. It is a religion, an experience, a oneness with nature. The more a golfer can come to terms with the metaphysical side of the sport, the better that golfer will golf.

Women golfers appreciate the natural beauty of their surroundings; they experience the course. They hear the birds, feel the wind, and smell the grass. The only natural beauty men golfers seek are birdies and eagles. Well, okay, they are also seekers. Yet they are not seekers of the cart path like women. They are seekers who seek to convert a golfer's paradise into an outdoor Las Vegas casino.

In essence, women play golf; men play craps. Betting and

golfing are synonymous for men. Four women golfers may agree that whoever scores highest net will buy the others a round of drinks. Four men golfers will bet five dollars each on whose ball is first on the green, first in the hole, and closest to the hole from a pitch—on each of the eighteen holes in a round. They will also make four five-dollar bets on the game: lowest gross, lowest net, lowest combination of scores, and most sandies. Finally, they will have four egos bet, one per player, eighteen times per game, on the length of their drives.

The weight of these bets weighs down the enjoyment of the game. In a casual game of golf, men play and cheat more by the rules than women players. Women golfers can afford to be kind. Their mortgage payment is not affected by it. Thus, if a woman shoots a ball out of bounds, her opponents will not require her to give up a stroke and distance. "Just drop a ball off to the side of the fairway," they tell her in unison.

Men golfers, on the other hand, expect their opponents to comply with this rule. They also, however, keep an extra ball in their own pocket to drop in the middle of a fairway after taking a long drive with a longer spin "just in case." The problem is that men are cheating when they do this, while women are merely being courteous. The path to greatness is a little easier when the rough part is already paved.

This is not to imply that all men are cheaters. Men just apply a different set of standards than we do. For instance, when women play with men, we just record all of our strokes. When men play with women they follow the 80 percent rule; that is, they record 80 percent of their hits. They do not bother taking any penalty strokes when they are playing with women. They think playing with women is enough of a penalty already. Now if it winds up that a woman finishes low gross, so be it. After all, men have ethics, too.

It is easy for us women to forget that. We think of ourselves as more honest and honorable because we are so much kinder than men on the course. It is easy, however, for women to be kind, because we structure our game differently. For instance, a woman golfer who is having a bad day can keep no score, or she can keep her score on only her good holes, or she can limit her score to a set number over par per hole. If a man is having a bad day, his playing buddies will turn to him as he leaves the par-4 green. "I'm sorry. I just could not keep track of all of your strokes. You were taking so many. Was that a nine or a ten for you?"

On the golf course, women get wise and men get whacked. In fact, the sad truth is that men golfers who are playing well get little attention from their foursome. Oh, they may get some compliments on their drives and some encouragement for their eagles. They are generally left alone to keep track of their own scores, however, with an occasional honesty check silently conducted by their opponents every two or three holes. A man with the double-bogey blues, however, is never left alone. His buddies will cackle at his incompetence and delight in his divots. "Are you having fun yet?" his best friend will crow.

This is not the case for the female foursome. A woman playing well keeps her own score. Her buddies rib her endlessly, though. "You never play like this when you are my partner," says one. "Yeah, pretty soon you will be too good to play with us," says another. The ribbing stops if she starts playing poorly. She can count on silence by her foursome. Silence—the call of the meditator. It is a gift. She can use it to improve her concentration. The silence will continue until she hits that first acceptable shot. "Great! You got your game back!" her friends exclaim.

So women meditate and mediate on the golf course, and men carry psychological clubs and cellular phones. The women have no fear. They can afford to ponder: Which came first—the ball or the hole? Men have to stay in touch. They may need to cash out their investment holdings if they are having a particularly bad day or their opponent is having a particularly good one.

Women play better golf because they *play*. Men, on the other hand, attack the game and each other with zeal instead of Zen.

Reason Five: Women take more lessons than men

Men golfers usually became golfers as youngsters. Perhaps they tagged along with their dad, maybe even caddied for him. By the time they took formal lessons, they already had consistency. They consistently swung poorly.

Most of us women golfers, on the other hand, were not junior golfers. We did not begin playing golf until we were in our twenties or thirties or even forties. In spite of this, we women are by far the superior players. At least part of the reason for our success is our training.

Obviously, anyone, male or female, whose IQ is higher than their score on an average round, has taken at least a few (hundred) lessons from a pro. Unlike most men, however, we women take at least one of those lessons before we go out on the golf course for the first time.

Men do not like to take golf lessons that cost less than one hundred dollars an hour. Why should they pay for some enhanced duffer to tell them what to do? Women golfers, on the other hand, bring a different set of values to golf. Every woman grew up taking lessons, whether they were dancing lessons, music lessons, charm lessons, or swimming lessons. Personal grace, endurance, and rhythm are, after all, more endearing assets to a ten-year-old girl than a mean dog or a fast punch. We women thus took lessons to develop these skills while we were growing up.

As a result, women golfers shift their weight well, have superior flexibility in their swings, and are actually willing to learn from a pro who has not yet achieved national recognition. For us women, lessons are a great complement (or, to be more honest, contradiction) to all of that coaching we receive. You know, the coaching so generously bestowed upon us by our husbands, boyfriends, and all of those many strangers we meet at the driving range who act as if any woman with a golf club is a damsel in distress needing testosterone, I mean, technical, assistance.

We women golfers thus play better than men. Men can thank the golf gods we are not elitists. Otherwise, we would not be so very willing to play golf with them.

Why Women Take Up Golf

Golf is not a game you grow into unless you started playing it when you were growing up. Most women thus choose to learn to golf.

Why? Why would we flirt with a hobby that is both more addictive and expensive than cocaine and more frustrating and fickle than a new boyfriend?

Why? Because the people who are important to us play. Why else? We take up golf so that we will have something to share with our husbands, or something to enjoy with our colleagues and clients, or some way to meet all of those attractive men on the golf course.

Do we admit that? Heck, no! Consider the plight of the married woman, the businesswoman, the single woman. It will then be easy to understand why.

Women Who Learn to Play Golf So They Can Play With Their Husbands

A married woman takes up golf when she notices that every Wednesday afternoon and Saturday morning her husband plays golf. Now, if these were his only absences, she would be glad to see him hit the sticks. She would then recognize it as a healthy form of stress relief for her and him. The problem is, however, that he is always absent—even when he is home.

Every night he is not at the driving range, her husband sits spellbound in front of the television. If she says something to him, he doesn't hear her. He is too absorbed. He is not an ordinary channel surfer, like many other men. He keeps their television on one channel. You guessed it. The golf channel.

Of course, he does not sit in front of their television all night, those evenings when he is home. He also attends to his yard work. He has to water that little putting green he put in the backyard. He carries a beeper with him when he goes outside to do this. He needs that beeper just in case he gets an important call. Maybe one of his golfing buddies will want to get in touch with him to see if he can round out a foursome.

When the couple has friends over, the conversation quickly turns from political debates and neighborhood news to hunting calls for eagles and birdies and spooky tales of the bad, bad bogey.

"All my husband ever thinks about is golf."

It's bad enough that the two do not share the same hobby. To speak different languages, however, is ridiculous!

Slowly she realizes, after years of denial, what this man considers important. He could not remember, the day after their wedding, who danced at their wedding reception. He could not remember, a year after their wedding, where they went on their honeymoon. He has perfect recall of every hole he ever has played, though, and how he scored on each of them.

Finally, one day she wakes up (alone). Her husband was lucky enough to get a 6:45 A.M. tee time. She decides she is going to save her marriage. She is going to learn to golf. She tells her husband when he gets home. He is delighted. He enthusiastically offers her his old clubs. He is going to teach her everything she needs to know.

The two of them head for the driving range. She has been there before. She is no stranger here. In fact, she has watched her husband strike ball after ball here before. Now, however, it is different. It is her turn. They are here so that she can learn to play.

Her husband adjusts her grip, shows her the approach, and tells her to keep her head down and her left arm stiff. He then proceeds to demonstrate the proper swing. He demonstrates it again and again. He keeps hitting her balls until he has hit the perfect shot.

Ah, finally. Now it is her turn to try. Whiff! Whiff! Smack! The ball rolls forward.

"You topped it," he explains.

She nods her head, acting as if this explanation is actually helpful. He shows her how to swing again. He keeps showing her how to swing until he hits the perfect ball. It takes him eleven times. Zoom! The ball goes flying.

"Your turn," he graciously says.

Whiff! Whiff! Smack! Another topped ball. Then another. Then another. Finally, one sails gracefully for twenty or thirty yards. It must be at least four or five inches off the ground!

She may slice. She, however, is hooked. "Wow! I really like this game!"

After several more trips to the range, she and her husband head out for the course. He hits his ball about 220 yards off the blue tee box, 190 of which is carry and 30 of which is roll. She hits her ball about 30 yards off the red tee box and then carries it with her in the golf cart about 160 yards as they ride to her husband's drive.

Her husband is happy. He has done a good job teaching his wife. She is learning to play the game right. She uses the red tee box. She picks up her ball upon command. She could play like this the rest of her life, and he would be satisfied. After all, if he wants some competition, he can play with the guys.

She is unhappy. She just is not good enough. She stops playing and rides with her husband for the last nine holes.

"Wow! This is even better!" he thinks.

How sad it is for her to recognize the truth. Her husband prefers to play with his regular foursome rather than with her. He has not invited her to one of his regular games. Not even when Billy was sick and they had a threesome. When she talks about her golf game at parties, he smiles, pats her on the back, and winks to his golf cronies. "Yeah, she's picking up the game very fast all right!" She decides she should take a few lessons from a pro. Maybe she will not even bother to mention it to her husband.

She starts off taking group lessons. They are inexpensive. There is even a class just for women. After three or four lessons, she stops getting that ache in her back and neck every time she hits a bucket of balls. Could it be because she is following her instructor's advice and not keeping her head stiffly down through every inch of the swing plane as her husband insisted she do?

Actually, she notices there is a funny thing about everything her husband told her about playing golf. His advice was a caricature of what a swing should be. He overemphasized every single uncomfortable angle. In fact, her husband never told her anything easy about golf. He never mentioned that the ball goes where you hit it. He focused on why the swing was unnatural and why she should feel unnatural doing it. No wonder she did not think she had any natural talent for it.

She meets other beginner golfers in her class. She starts golfing with them. After all, she and her husband are not golfing together on Saturday morning or on Wednesday after work. Her new friends do not give her constant instruction, as her husband did. They concentrate on their own game instead. They enjoy themselves. She does, too.

She finally gets rid of her husband's old clubs. She finds some that fit her so that she actually has a shot at making a good shot. She now is ready to play with her husband. Yet she is too caught up with her own foursome. She likes the laughter and friendly competition she enjoys with the other women.

She has, in fact, played with many women golfers who are better than her husband. She realizes that her husband may think, eat, and breathe golf, but he really does not play golf very well. His etiquette is atrocious. He is always giving unwelcome tips to other players (e.g., her). His swing plane is far from classic. He has no understanding of golf rules. He is always telling her to pick up her ball. Furthermore, he just does not fit in with her crowd. They play from the red tees.

She has become a golfer. Sooner or later, someone will ask her why. Unless the person is a really good friend or the woman is unusually honest, she will not admit she took up the sport to get close to her husband. She has, after all, learned a lot about this game.

She has learned that to get within twenty strokes of her husband's handicap she has had to spend three hours each week, for three years, hitting three buckets of balls, and she has had to spend $3,000 on golf lessons. Just how self-actualized is she, if she did all this to spend four or five hours, once or twice a month, for five or six months a year with a man? In fact, not just *a* man, but the very man who had already promised he would spend the rest of his life with her anyway! No, unless you and this woman are really close friends or unless she is unusually honest, she probably will not admit that she took up golf solely so that she can share that experience with her husband.

"Oh, I wanted to get some exercise. Plus I thought it was something I could do with my husband," she will say. Right! As if riding around in a golf cart all day makes your heart beat faster than walking around the mall with an amount of spending money equivalent to your greens fees.

Perhaps she may say instead, "My husband golfs so much, and he always raved about how great it was to be outdoors all day. I wanted a bit of that fresh air and sunshine myself." Of course, you know that she always spends ten minutes applying 40 SPF lotion on every visible body part. That way the portion of air carrying sunshine just sort of slides off her greasy skin.

This does not mean that golf does not add to her marriage. Married women golfers engage with their spouses in pillow talk of birdies and eagles and those elusive holes in one, even if they do usually play with friends other than their mates.

Many women learn golf to play with their husbands. They should not be ashamed. After all, they *play* the game entirely for themselves.

Women Who Learn to Play Golf So They Can Play With Colleagues and Clients

Now consider the woman who wants to learn golf to enhance her business relationships. A businesswoman takes up golf after she wakes up one morning and realizes that just maybe having a 20 handicap would be better for her career than getting a Harvard MBA. Some event will trigger her awakening. Perhaps she was abandoned at some country club pool when all of her associates teed off during a business meeting. Perhaps she became annoyed when she realized it was acceptable to take off early and golf with a colleague, but unacceptable to leave the office to go shopping with one. More likely, she realizes playing golf is more than a sport. It is also a political statement. It loudly announces, "I fit in."

To be politically successful in the corporate sector you must play golf. Yet effective office politics demand that one appear apolitical. This is troubling, because everyone this woman now wants to play golf with knows she does not know how to play. Everyone also knows that in order for her to get her game up to even double-bogey status, she will have to spend more hours learning the game than she works overtime and more dollars on pro fees than her last two annual bonuses combined.

So why would this woman admit she spent all of this time and money learning the game so that she could play with her boss once next year at the annual golf outing? Her colleagues would probably think she had more personal integrity if, instead of worrying about Saturday play, she just changed religions and joined her boss's church for Sunday service.

Thus, though a businesswoman is driven to drive the same way she is driven to success, she pretends she is indulging in the sport for other than business reasons. In her mind, all she needs to become the CEO is to click her cleats together and follow the cart path of the course. Yet she tells her colleagues something else. "I thought I would give golf a try. Everyone else seems to like it. Plus my husband really loves to play. And I could use some sort of activity to relieve the stress from all of the long hours I have been putting in around the office lately."

A businesswoman initially will pretend she has only a mild interest in the sport. Yet every businesswoman who takes up golf takes it up wholeheartedly. Money is no object and time is merely a commodity. If she does not invest immediately in a five-day golf school, she will at least take some lessons from a local pro. She will buy the best clubs available from the local pro shop. Businesswomen practice regularly. They visualize success. They love every part of the sport, particularly the part that they hope will lead to a promotion.

The beginning woman golfer usually also joins a businesswomen's league a few months after she starts whacking balls at the range. They play a lot of scrambles. She can thus get her game in shape before she starts playing with the businessmen with whom she associates.

A year or two later, however, she decides networking with the ladies brings a lot more personal and career growth opportunities than playing with the guy in the next office. After all, she and her colleague are competing for clients. These female executives, however, could become her clients.

This does not mean she has not putted her way into playing with the big guys at the office. Maybe she has invited one to a charity golf event. Perhaps she has invited a couple of clients and a colleague to play at her club. Maybe she has even hooked her way into being paired up with the boss at the annual corporate golf outing.

The problem, however, is that the businesswoman golfer generally accepts golf into her life much faster than her colleagues will accept her into their game. A woman may discover that the barrier between her and her associates is more than whether or not she can play golf. It is even more than whether or not she can play golf well. The barrier may be whether or not she can play golf with them. Will they even extend an invitation?

In the course of time, she can expect her peers to welcome her on the course. Ultimately, however, it is not businessmen who decide with whom the woman golfer plays; she makes that decision herself. Like the average male executive, she wants to play in a foursome of golfers who are successful, career oriented, and serious about the game. Oh, yeah, it helps if they have high voices, too.

Women Who Learn to Play Golf to Meet Men

Women who take up golf to meet men are originally more interested in tall, dark, and handsome than long, straight, and true. These women take a few lessons, buy some secondhand clubs, and as soon as they can hit fifty yards, they hit the links.

A woman on the prowl never goes to a golf course alone. When a golfer goes to a course alone, the starter will usually pair her up with a threesome or with a twosome and one other lone player. At many courses, when conducting the pairing, the starter will yell out the name of the lead golfer in each group and the number of the people in that golfer's party. Thus, if Mary Smith goes to the course alone and the starter wants to pair her up with the Murphy party of three, there's a very high probability the starter will shout, "Murphy threesome with Smith Single." She just would feel too desperate to be paired up by a starter who announced her surname to the world as "Single."

Thus, a single woman on the lookout usually starts out going to courses as part of a female twosome. This means that she will never get to ride or walk with the men she came to meet. Instead she will spend her four-and-a-half hours on the course with the woman with whom she arrived.

She does not care, though. Usually she spends so much time talking to the woman she came with that she later does not remember even the name of the handsome guy who is playing with them by the third hole. Plus, the more she plays, the more she likes—and concentrates—on the game itself.

She also has noticed that the men they are paired up with are not terribly receptive toward her anyway. Somehow they can spot right off that she is a new golfer—even when she drives her ball one hundred yards. One of them may ask her why she has taken up the sport. What is she supposed to say? The truth? "I want to get married and thought I would have a better chance meeting a guy golfing than at a singles bar. After all, I do have much less competition out here." No, of course she cannot say this. She responds, "Women really have to know how to play. It is just part of the realities of the business world we live in."

The only thing that becomes second nature to her sooner than this little white lie is her love for the little white ball. The more she plays, the better she gets, and the more she enjoys herself.

After a while, a woman golfer who takes up golf to meet a man goes to the course to play golf instead. She usually becomes part of a regular female foursome. She then has no chance of ever meeting a man on the tee box again. She has found something better, though: herself and her swing.

Second Hole

All Golfers Are Not Equally Handicapped

The Sexism of the Clock

Time is relative. Einstein himself said so.

He may have been a golfer, too. The relativity of time is most obvious on the golf course—especially when people who use the white tees are playing with people who use the red tees. There's no sense hiding behind the tee colors, though, in an effort to be politically correct. We all have heard it. Men say women play slow golf. Men say this when they are playing with women. They say this when they are playing behind women. They say this under all circumstances—except, of course, when the women behind them are approaching too quickly. Then they say women have poor golf etiquette.

Not all men say women play slowly for the same reasons. Like time, the reasons given are relative. The reasons depend on the relative physical location of the men and women golfers to each other.

The Man–Woman Combo

Consider the clock calculations of the man who is playing with a woman. The first time-waster the man perceives is at the very, very beginning of the game. It is at the first tee. There is in fact, no longer a first tee. There are two first tees. There are the white or blue tees and then there are the red tees. In other words, there are the tees from which the real golfers play, and then there are the tees from which the women golfers attempt to drive.

This is not the only extra stop a man must make on the first hole. There is also that extra stop 175 yards straight down the middle of the fairway from the red tees. This is where the woman has driven her ball.

"Not a bad shot," he admits. Yet he looks at his watch and wishes he could keep going. He wants to go over to the trees on the right in the distance. That's where his drive went.

"Boy, oh boy, that baby must have gone 250 yards. Might be tough to find but I can't afford to waste a great drive like that," he muses. "What a great ball!"

When the woman (finally) hits her ball, and it is safe for him to get on his way, he proceeds over to the out-of-bounds area. Always interested in fast play, he jumps out of his cart or, if walking, sets up his bag stand quickly. Then he spends about five minutes selecting several clubs from his bag.

"I'm shooting a black Titleist," he announces to the woman he is playing with as he begins to search for his ball. Why couldn't I be playing with a man? he silently wonders. Then he probably would have to be looking in this area, too.

There are a few balls in the rough. Most of them were left by women players, who do not usually have a half hour to look for their misspent shots. A Pinnacle is closest out; then there is a Flying Lady stuck down in the bottom of a creek he did not realize was there. He finally comes across a black Titleist. It is lodged behind a large maple tree.

"That Titleist can't be mine," he says. "I know my ball didn't go this far back. Looks like the wrong number anyway."

Then he remembers. He has played with Pinnacles before. That ball with the close out, the one nearest the fairway—that ball must be his!

"I found it," he yells to his golf mate, who he believes has quite rudely abandoned the search for his ball and walked over to hers. Fifteen minutes after he began searching the woods, he hauls off and hits that sucker low. Really low. Punches it out. With his foot.

"With her pansy drives, we gotta bend the rules a little bit for fast play," he mutters to himself.

Two hits later, both players are on the green. She tries to make a 6-foot putt; the ball misses the hole. It is now two feet on the other side of its target.

He measures his ball and the green from every possible angle; he wants to make his needed 4-foot putt. "Women say men can't putt," he says. "We'll see about that!"

He bends down on all fours; he then stands behind his ball, squinting, hemming and hawing. He calculates the read of the green with apparent grass-splitting precision. He putts; his ball rolls around the edge of the hole and stops three inches outside it. He picks up the ball quickly.

"You are going to have to pick up," he explains, pointing to the people 450 yards back on the tee box. "We don't want to hold them up."

They walk back to the cart. Oh, well, he thinks, I guess she didn't slow us down too much. Oh, well, she thinks, I guess I can't expect him to play as well as my league friends just because he's a man.

Men in the Rear

Let's look at another scenario. Let's see what happens when men golfers are playing behind women golfers.

In this circumstance, the men notice on the first tee that there has been some kind of mistake. A group of women golfers is in front of them. This obviously is not their lucky day, and it is going to be a very long day, too.

"Maybe we can cut ahead," an optimistic man offers.

They watch the women approach the red tees. Why, the women are just standing there, practicing their swing strokes, chatting casually!

"What are they waiting for, they oughtta go now," one of the men trumpets as he notices the group in front of the women are 200 yards down the fairway. "No way those women can hit that far!" he proclaims. Wasted, wasted time.

The women tee off. All of the men simultaneously reach the same conclusion. The women's balls just don't go very far. They *do* go farther down the fairway from the red tees than half of the men's balls will go from the white tees, but no one knows that yet. The proof will be gone shortly, anyway.

So the men roll their eyes at one another, put their hands on their hips, and begin to practice the stare they intend to give the women all afternoon, until they let them pass through. "Boy, oh boy," one says, "these women are already slowing things down."

Eventually, on the sixth hole, a par-3, they come to a screeching halt. It was inevitable. They had women in front of them and now they are backed up, stalled, stuck on the golf course.

The women do not even acknowledge they are at fault. When the men ask if they can play through, the women say they can later, but only when there is a place for them to go. Right now, the women point out, they are playing faster than the all-male group in front of them, and that is why the eight of them are now waiting to play.

The men know better, however. They know a basic male truth. Someplace on this course, maybe too far ahead for them to see, but someplace on this course, there is another woman playing—and that woman is slowing things down.

Women in the Rear

The last combination in which men and women interface on the golf course is when women golfers are behind men golfers. The first thing men think when they see this combination is that this is their lucky day.

They don't think about it again unless and until the women golfers behind them are getting a little too close to them. Maybe— heaven forbid—the women even hit a ball into them—or to fifty yards or so behind them. In that situation, every man will come to grips with the reality of the speed of play. Not all women golfers play slow. It is just the ones ahead of them who do.

The Difference Between Men and Women Golfers

The Difference Between Men and Women Golfers Who Have Never Picked Up a Golf Club

Women who don't know how to play golf say they do not know how to play golf. Men who don't know how to play golf explain they can no longer play due to a significant football or basketball injury.

The Difference Between Men and Women Beginning Golfers

A Beginning Woman Golfer	*A Beginning Man Golfer*
Wears a bracelet to keep track of how many strokes she has hit	Adds his strokes mentally or takes a double bogey—whichever is less
Explains the first time she plays that this is her first time	Explains the first time he plays that he usually plays much better
Wears shirts and shorts with pictures of lady golfers or tees and balls	Forgets collar rule and wears T-shirt
Takes group classes with other women	Takes solo lessons from male pro
Makes lots of beginning women golfer friends	Makes friends with men who say they usually play much better than they play when they play with him

The Difference Between Men and Women Intermediate Golfers

An Intermediate Woman Golfer	*An Intermediate Man Golfer*
Has enough confidence to play with only men	Is sometimes willing to play with only women
Could play comfortably from the white tees but chooses the red	Could play comfortably from the white tees but chooses the blue
Turns her scorecard in every time she plays or at least every time she plays well	Turns his scorecard in every time he plays or at least every time he plays poorly
Wears sophisticated, yet casual golf clothing, some of which bear the name of her league or country club	Wears golf shirt that sports the name of a course that is much more expensive than the one he is playing
Can drive	Can putt
Credits her success to lessons and perseverance	Credits his success to natural talent

The Difference Between Women Pro Golfers and Men Pro Golfers

Women pro golfers get old. Men pro golfers become seniors.

Why Men Don't Like to Be Paired Up With Women

Men golfers generally do not like to be paired up with women golfers they don't know. We all know the scenario. It's a beautiful spring afternoon. You've been able to cut out of work early enough to get in at least nine holes. None of your friends is free. You go to the course yourself. You know the starter will pair you up with someone. You hope it is someone who doesn't play a lot better than you.

The starter takes your name; you wait to be called. You start to contemplate the worst. What if you are paired up with three guys who shoot in the seventies? Why aren't there any other women here?

You hear your name. You head out to the tee.

You see your new golf buddies. Oh, no. You noticed these guys inside. They are serious golfing men. In the pro shop, they spoke to each other and avoided eye contact with you. They were hoping, very obviously hoping, that they would not be paired up with you. You walk up, shake hands, and introduce yourself.

The older gentleman smiles. "I didn't know I was going to get to play with a pretty lady," he says.

Charming as he is, you know the truth. Men do not like to be paired up with women on the golf course. They will even admit it, when they are not in the process of being paired up with you. You wonder why men see this as such an unusual coupling. Men, you discover, give various reasons as to why they do not like to play with women.

Speed of Play

All golfers have some concerns about speed of play. A male golfer, however, has special concerns when he is paired up with a woman. What if she plays much faster than he does? What if she cannot hit the ball at all?

Many men are convinced that the only women on the golf course are the ones who just finished their first golf lesson last week. They do not have that concern when they are paired up with an unknown man.

They have, after all, played before with men who beat them. They have never played with a woman who has beaten them, though. Okay, maybe that is not true. Those times when a woman did win, though, it was only because they were having a very, very bad day, an exceptionally bad day that was so unusual there is no reason to even mention it. Plus she cheated anyway—she *had* to have cheated.

One would think that if men were truly concerned about speed of play, they would ask each player assigned to their foursome his or her handicap. When a man is paired up with a woman, though, he does not care about her handicap. He is too worried about his own handicap. Not the one on his scorecard—he is concerned about that emotional disability he sustains whenever some woman sees him hit his usual slice. He foresees that once again he is going to get caught—caught in the act and practice of being a duffer. Men think all women believe men are good golfers, or at least better than they are. It's a pedestal that men don't want to fall off.

Men correctly point out that their swing speeds are faster than women's. However, speed of play is very slightly affected by the speed of a single swing. The activity between the strokes determines course speed. Since women are such excellent time managers, they play much faster than men. If you do not believe that, then compare what the average man does in a day (goes to work) to what the average woman does in a day (goes to work; cooks; arranges family social schedule; cares for home, children, man, pets, and relatives). If the woman makes it to the golf course, that fact alone shows she is the superior time manager. There is no rational reason for a man's belief that a woman will play slowly. Moreover, even if the woman is a good player—a fast player—a man still may not want to play with her.

Talking About Business Matters and Making Important Business Contacts

Men say golf is a major networking device. Thus they would much rather be paired up with that nineteen-year-old male wearing sneakers and jeans with a hole in the seat than the forty-five-year-old female executive standing next to him. Yes, by golly! That young fellow is the one who is going to help them land a $500,000 contract with the company where she works!

A male reader, of course, will be quick to point out how ridiculous this logic is; after all, the guy about to be paired up doesn't know where she works. That, however, is precisely the point!

If networking were the issue, the man who showed up at a course would be indifferent to whether his potential partner was male or female. (After all, female golfers generally are very successful in the business world.) He would engage in conversation with potential participants and find out what they did and where they worked. Then he could try to be paired up with the ones who might someday help him in his career. Men don't do that, though. Instead, they look at the pool of players and use a mental checklist to determine with whom they want to play.

"Let's see. Penis? Yeah, he's okay."

"No penis? Sorry, but I want to play fast today."

Furthermore, despite their professed intentions, men don't talk about important business matters on the golf course. At least, men who know golf etiquette don't. Golfing is a way to get to know the people you do business with. You may intend to engage in business afterward. Golf, however, is merely an acceptable way to court that business.

Finally, people with important business matters to discuss on the golf course also usually have the foresight to arrange a foursome and a tee time. How serious is the business of some self-professed rainmaker, if he can't even find two colleagues to join him when he is with his client?

Golf As a Male Bonding Ritual

Male bonding is the weakest excuse of them all. Women golfers share intimacies on the golf course; men golfers share their beer. Intimacy between men on the golf course consists of a quick rundown of number of children, number of wives, and the numbers of their favorite holes on this and other golf courses.

Men who want to bond with other males buy drums and beat music together in a male-only group. Men who want to tell dirty jokes, make fun of women, and call each other "Olive" after each lousy shot, buy clubs and golf together in a male-only group.

Men thus do not like being paired up with women on a golf course. Yet there is no valid reason for their displeasure. Women, though they obviously have excellent reasons for not wanting to play with men, are willing to play with anyone.

Men vs. Women Winter Golfers

Every golfer loves a stolen winter's day. That's the kind of day when the temperature is twenty to thirty degrees, the wind is quietly howling, the ground is dry, the sun is shining, and you are going golfing. Okay, the weather may not be perfect, but this may be the very last chance that you have to play golf this winter. You are not going to miss it!

There's a casual side to winter golf. You do not have to book your tee time nine days in advance. You can just show up unscheduled at the club. As long as it is not closed because of the weather, you can get on right away.

This does not mean winter golf is a spur-of-the-moment opportunity. In winter golf, the whole success of the game depends on adequate preparation. Now, I am not talking about hitting a bucket or two of balls from the driving range before you play. After all, it is cold outside. You would have to be some kind of idiot to stand around and hit a bunch of little white balls that you didn't intend to chase after.

No, you prepare differently for winter golf than you do for summer golf. For starters, you must bring the proper equipment. Golf cart users bring detachable windshields just in case they happen to get a cart which does not have one. Golfers who walk the course bring brandy and hot chocolate. What counts even more than equipment in winter golf, however, is your wardrobe.

Women golfers have a competitive advantage in winter golf. After our divorce from uncomfortable, toe-pinching high heels in the sixties, few women today need to be reminded how important comfort is. It is socially acceptable for us to admit to feeling cold, so we do everything we can to avoid being unpleasantly chilled. A woman golfer wears earmuffs or a wool hat, silk and cotton thermals, Gore-Tex pants and a sweatshirt, an extra-heavy-duty windbreaker, one pair of warm golf gloves, and, between strokes, a pair of mittens. Men, on the other hand, think of themselves as too macho to get cold. They thus show up on the course with a single summer golf glove, a golf hat, a sweatshirt, and a light windbreaker.

The woman golfer talks about how wonderful it is to get out on the course, how they must be nuts to be out there, how very cold it is but why she is not, and how she hopes she will have another chance to play before spring. The man golfer talks about how cold he is, how more clothing would have interfered with his swing, and why it might be a really good idea if they knocked off before they finished this round. He is starting to worry about getting frostbite on his ears.

We women have more than the advantage of being warm in the winter. There is also a substantial difference in winter versus summer golf rules. In winter, you can play your ball up. This means you can improve the lie of your ball if, for instance, it ends up on a patch of ground with no grass. This makes a big difference to the average woman golfer's game, because she has trouble getting under the ball in such circumstances. This same rule, however, actually hurts the average man's game—particularly if he is playing with a woman with a similar handicap. This is because most men always improve their lie anyway. Under winter rules, it is no longer a competitive advantage, as his opponents are doing the same thing.

Informal custom also dictates different standards for winter versus summer scoring. Whiffs and mulligans are overlooked by both men and women golfers in the winter. After all, it is cold outside. It is in everyone's interest to move this game along. Winter golf is like a marathon. Completion of the course is itself a victory and no one is going to mind a fast participant. Winter scoring is thus more a matter of personal attitude than stroke measurement: "I'll take a 5" or "Give me a par." Such personal assessments may or may not measure up to actual performance. Yet no one cares. Even men do not bet heavily in the winter.

Women golfers play well in winter. We enjoy the game more than men do. We shiver quietly as we tell each other jokes about the ice forming in our bangs. Then we line up to bang our balls as far as we can down the fairway. "Maybe our balls will get more roll in the ice!" we tell each other as we slip on one more layer of clothing to protect ourselves against the elements.

Usually we women golfers do not get too cold to play until about the fifteenth hole. What kind of golfer, however, would stop playing that close to the end? Maybe a man, but certainly not a woman! No, we women finish our games. Then we warm up at the nineteenth hole with cordial memories of the few good shots we had. Men golfers usually leave the nineteenth hole wishing for spring. When it is time for us to leave, however, we women agree there is only one thing we would need to get us to say it was a perfect world—one more stolen winter's day.

Handicap Arithmetic—The Difference Between the Sexes

Some people think the biggest difference between a man with a 15 handicap and a woman with a 15 handicap is about 108 yards. That length, of course, does not represent the yardage differences between the red and white tees. No, the 108 yards represents the eighteen six-foot gimmes that the average male with a 15 handicap takes per round of golf.

This is the case, however, only when the man golfer, in his perception, honestly records his strokes. Less honest men with a 15 handicap play much better than their handicap indicates. Unlike us women, men golfers have conquered the oldest golfing tradition of all—sandbagging. So, the next time you compete with a man who has a handicap identical to yours, rest assured that the real difference between your play will be about nine strokes. The only problem is you won't know in whose favor until the bets are in!

If You See the Golf Guru, Club Him

The average woman thinks she cannot practice or play golf without encountering at least one man who wants to tell her how to use her clubs. The exception to this, of course, is when she is in a coed golfing lesson. Then the pro will spend only one-quarter of the time with her that he spends with his male students. In order for us to understand why we women get so much attention when we do not want it, and so little when we do, we must examine what happens when we go to the driving range or the golf course. Only then can we hope to induce men to change their behavior toward us.

On the Range

Let's think of what happens when we go to the driving range. Every woman golfer who has ever gone to the range to "get away from it all" has instead found it all there—in the hungry faces of men starving to give some instruction.

When that man on the next tee box starts talking to you about your game, he is not making a pass at you. He is just trying to improve your game by passing on a tip or two. He might, for instance, explain that he just happened to notice your swing plane is crooked; your grip is too weak; and you are coming up a little bit in your backswing. He may then end his recital with a humble smile. "The only reason I noticed was because I used to do the same thing."

He has made this last remark to make you feel better. You are not hitting the ball poorly; you are merely hitting the ball as poorly as he did before he became the good player he is today. You are making mistakes that this very kind stranger with the terrible slice already has corrected in his game. Why, his current slice must be due to a totally different set of reasons...presumably much more acceptable ones!

You would like this man to change his behavior toward you, yet you do not want to tell him to mind his own business. His intentions, after all, are admirable. Moreover, you may be sub-consciously signaling that you want help. Even pros who charge for their lessons—or should—will often stop by a struggling woman golfer (even if she just happens to drive her ball 200 yards) to tell her what she is doing wrong.

For instance, I used to visit a range where the local pro charged men thirty dollars for a thirty-minute lesson. Since I was one of his few female patrons, however, he felt compelled to offer me some free advice on the tee box. At first I was absolutely delighted by his attention. I would pay for a six-dollar bucket of balls and get about sixty dollars worth of advice. I decided not to tell any of my friends of my good fortune. After all, if business picked up too much, he would not have the time or inclination to help me.

After fifteen to twenty visits to that range, however, I started to become embarrassed. I felt a little cheap. He must think I am taking advantage of him, I worried. To ease my guilty conscience, I began buying the eight-dollar bucket. Now I was getting sixty dollars worth of advice for eight dollars. That seemed *much* more fair.

At least, that seemed much more fair for a little while. Then I started getting that guilty conscience again. Maybe I should sign up to take a couple of lessons from him, I thought. He must think I am such a sponge.

It just didn't seem right for me to pay for lessons from him then, though. Once I started paying for tips he gave me during formal lessons, would he expect me to tip him every time he voluntarily stopped by to tell me to swish my hips? What impact would all of this have on our business relationship? I wondered. I did not want to ruin a good thing.

After ten more visits to the range, I became less concerned about creating some change. I was also not at all concerned about our relationship. He was quickly becoming a pain in the neck—a pain that was even worse than all of the physical aches and pains I normally get from golfing. He is constantly intruding into my practice sessions, I thought. Heck! If I wanted someone to critique every swing, I would be taking lessons, not just hitting balls at a driving range. I even broke my vow of secrecy and began to complain to my friends about him. "Wow!" one of them exclaimed. "Free lessons all of the time! I'm going to start going there, too!"

With five to ten more visits to that range behind me I still have not seen any of my friends there. I really dislike this pro now. He, on the other hand, has become even more comfortable with our relationship. Familiarity has crept in on him. I am part of his extended golfing family. The old rules of customer and business-man no longer apply. He doesn't feel compelled, as he once did, to stop by and politely point out every one of my flawed finishes.

Heck! he figures. I'm not charging her for these lessons. I'll just yell out the pro shop door every time she does something wrong! That will be a lot easier.

So he does. I hit a slice and his voice booms across the range. "Watch your backswing and hit the ball in-out! In-out! In-out! Remember: in-out." (I glance around quickly. This could be subject to misinterpretation. I hope my husband isn't here.)

My next ball qualifies for competition at the local bowling alley. "Stay down! Keep your head down! Stop coming up!" he shouts.

Pretty soon the men around me start giving him and me dirty looks. How are they supposed to concentrate when my lousy swings are being broadcast?

"This is unbelievable," I say to one of the men. "I wish he would knock it off."

The man next to me is suddenly empathetic. He feels sorry for me. He realizes that this is not my fault.

He says, "Let me give you a little bit of advice. If he is giving you a lesson, he should be standing right next to you; otherwise, you are not really getting your money's worth. Now I wouldn't have noticed, but I took a lesson from him once and I was not the least bit satisfied." He then asks me, "Do you want to know what I would do if I were you?"

I am so astonished that this man thinks I am actually paying for this verbal-abuse broadcast, I do not recover quickly enough to answer him.

"Well, I'll tell you what I would do," he continues. "I would move that ball back a little bit further in my stance and keep my back a little straighter..."

On the Course

Women, of course, do not get free lessons only on the range. Since men never read the golf books their wives buy them every Christmas, they are unaware of expert opinion that golfers should not try to change their swing on the course. Thus they see no problem with telling women golfers everything they should change during their play.

For a woman to get free advice, it is not necessary, of course, for her actually to be playing with a man. Often men playing near you will oblige you with a lesson.

Once I was right in the middle of my waggle when I heard a ball fall about ten yards to my left. Those guys behind us are out of their minds! I thought as I quickly turned around to give them a piece of my mind. No one was on that tee box, though. Then, off to my right, I saw a man jumping over a ditch, then darting in and around a grove of trees; he began to wave smartly at me with his 5-wood. "Are you sure that's your ball?" he yelled in an incriminating voice. "I just hit one over here."

"That must be your ball over there," I answered, as I pointed to the ball that almost hit me on the head. He briskly walked over to the ball and inspected it to make sure it was his ball.

I then realized that he intended to hit his ball before I hit mine. He also planned to hit his ball over me and over the creek and forest that separated our fairways. I started to move away. I was heading for the left side of my fairway and a safe distance behind him.

"Oh, no," he said. "You are fine where you are."

Sure! As if there were no chance that this man whose last shot went about seventy degrees off course could possibly make a five-degree deviation in intended direction or height on this swing!

"I'm sure I'm okay, but I'll get out of your way anyway," I courteously replied.

He hit his ball. He was right. That ball would have missed me by a mile. In fact, it hit one of the highest branches on one of the tallest trees and then abruptly fell into the creek.

I raised my eyebrows in an "Oh, well" expression and then walked over to my ball. Maybe I'll hit a practice swing first, I thought. The man stopped to watch me as I did. "Not bad," he said. "But you really shouldn't go that far back in your backswing if you want to keep control."

Ladies, I figured out what our problem is. I know why men stand in line to point out a tip or two we may (or may not) use. The problem is men know we keep ourselves too much under control.

We never throw a club on the course, and we never throw a fit in their face. The next time you meet a golf guru, club him. You will be doing the rest of us a favor.

The Good Guys

It's easy to make generalizations about men golfers versus women golfers. We must recognize, however, that as with all generalizations, there are a number of exceptions. In fact, my fairway research, which even the Internal Revenue Service will agree was quite extensive, indicates that the generalizations set forth in this book are true only about 80 percent of the time. Not all men cheat on their scores, lie about their lies, or steal as many victories as they win. Only 80 percent of them do.

Let's hear it for the good guys! The good guys are as much, if not more, fun to play with or around (or play around with) as any woman golfer.

Who are the good guys? They are the men who create golfing opportunities for the women with whom they work. They are the guys who suggest Suzy or Sally should golf in the Wednesday afternoon game.

The good guys are the men who really like to play with women. I have one friend who goes out of his way to be paired up with a woman golfer. "Women are fun to play with," he explains. "They laugh at all of my jokes and at only their own mistakes. They

"She won't let me win at golf."

seldom gibe me when my game is off. They are less uptight than men about the game."

The good guys are the men who like to play golf in a foursome consisting of themselves and three women. Usually, a man enters this foursome arrangement via his wife's invitation. (Even starters usually are not that cruel.) The good guy and his wife will ride in one cart; the two other women in another. All four players, however, share the game and the afternoon. The only fifth wheel in this foursome is the marshal, who stares in amazement as he occasionally drives by.

What about the man who takes up golf because his wife or girlfriend suffers from the golfing bug? He is always a good guy. You can tell by watching him. Just look for the couple with the woman who keeps telling her husband what to do. Maybe she will point out why he whiffed his last shot. Maybe she will tell him his backswing is too fast. "Don't try to kill the ball," you will hear her remind him as she triple bogeys the hole. "Okay," he will mutter as he good-naturedly takes another shot at it. Men who are learning golf to play with their wives usually learn to play in spite of them.

Finally, the good guys are those men who are just fun to play around. For instance, one time when I was playing a beautiful course in west Texas, my female threesome caught up with the male twosome in front of us when we reached the par-3 signature hole. The men waved brightly to us when they left the green and courteously sped up their play. We never saw them again. How we each wished we had, though! We wanted to thank them for the souvenir they left behind for us. The first one of us to pocket her ball in the hole found it. Those guys had left us a bright pink ball. That put them one notch above the rest. They were officially good guys in our golf book.

A man does not have to be a good golfer to be a good guy. A good guy can lose his ball on a sliced drive or four-putt on a green the same way as his socially challenged male counterpart does. The difference is not in what he does, but what he then does *not* do. When he has one or more bad shots, he does not claim the woman in his group is throwing his game off. He does not throw his clubs. He does not threaten to give up the game. He does not call himself a jerk so that the others in his foursome feel as if they are walking on pins and needles rather than fairways and greens. He just concentrates on getting his game back or, in more serious cases, developing one.

Many good guys are, of course, good golfers. A good guy who is a good golfer does not belittle his opponents in conversation or conduct. He never offers a tip unless someone asks his advice. He does, however, encourage all of the golfers with whom he plays to play their best. In fact, he may bet his female opponent that she will shave at least five points off her handicap by the end of the season.

A good guy likes playing with good golfers—men and women. A good guy doesn't think it is unfair when, due to tee placements, a woman outdrives him on the course but not in actual yardage. He accepts the parameters of the course as much as he welcomes a woman who hits her balls long and straight—even if she just happens to hit them longer and straighter than he does, yard for yard. The good guys delight in a woman's good scores.

Even a good guy, however, will label a women who breaks one hundred an exceptional golfer and a man who does not a hacker. Is it such a bad thing, though, to be admired for mediocrity?

There is only one thing better than playing with a good guy. That is, of course, being married to one.

Third Hole

The Science of the Swing

Golf 101: Swing Classics

There is more to golf than hitting a ball long and straight. If you really want to impress the heck out of your friends, you need a strong grip, a bar-stool posture, an ergonomically sound swing plane, and, most important, some distinctive tweak. A distinctive tweak sets you apart from the ordinary hacker. It is your best proof that it took more than a five-day golf school to mess up your swing. It took more than a bunch of pros. It took you.

We golfers, of course, are sort of like tomcats. We can put our creative mark in any number of places. Yet there will always be some human who will come along when we do and say we should not have put it there. Keep sniffing, though, and eventually you find some territory you can confidently mark as your own.

For instance, consider the grip. The experts will tell you there are all kinds of grips. There are Vardon grips, baseball grips, overlapping grips, regular grips, strong grips, weak grips, loose grips, and pressurized grips. There are so many types of grips that it is hard to get a grip on them all. When you give it some thought, there are only two kinds of grips, though. There are correct grips and there are incorrect grips.

Correct grips are the way the pros teach us to hold our clubs. A correct grip is easy to learn. Seventy-five percent of all beginners who have had ten or more lessons grip their clubs correctly.

Then there are incorrect grips. Incorrect grips are simply correct grips with adjustments. Incorrect grips are the grips 100 percent of all beginning golfers and 90 percent of all other golfers assume after they reposition their hands from their correct grips so that they can actually swing their clubs.

Bad grips are as natural on the golf course as putters are in putt-putt golf. No golfer ever need try to individualize her grip. It already is unique.

Your manner of addressing the ball is a better place to set yourself, as well as your feet, apart. Men generally have better golf posture than women. All that time they spend developing their "bar stool behinds" really pays off. Most women, on the other hand, have a tendency to keep their seats tucked in when they stand over their golf balls.

One way to develop some class on the golf course, therefore, is to stick your rear end out. This focus on keeping your butt out does more than help your swing. It's an effective reminder. It is much better than a string around your finger, because it is symbolic. What should you say to the friendly man in your foursome who offers you some advice about your address? Ahh, remember? "Butt out! Butt out!"

Don't let anyone convince you, though, that the only opportunity for eccentricity in your address is the way you moon the golfers in your foursome. There is also posture and ball placement.

Pros say your posture should change along with your club selection. This does not mean you should go from standing tall, looking confident, and keeping your back straight when you pull out an 8-iron to slouching, slumping your shoulders, and rounding your back when someone hands you your driver. Sure, it is true that a man golfer changes his posture to match the height of his ego during his most recent club selection process. A woman golfer, however, is advised to fit her posture to her respective club's length instead.

It also is helpful to know that most golfers stand too close to their balls. What golfer does not want to get close and personal with her ball? There is always an excellent chance you may hit it and never see it again. Yet pros say that, in fact, the longer the club you are using, the farther you should stand away from your ball.

You can individualize your game successfully by keeping some distance from your ball. Stretching for your ball is a wonderful way to show off. Everyone will know you must be at least as limber as a flexible graphite shaft to reach *that* distance. Also, this stance creates extra time in your life. You can stop taking those yoga lessons.

Stretching for your ball gives a creative opportunity to the men you play with. They do not have to give you that hackneyed advice about keeping your head down. "Keep your heels down!" they will proudly yell. What the heck, they think, maybe someone will hear them. This is, after all, no cookie-cutter instruction.

The problem with this individualizing strategy, however, is that you run the risk that only men who pride themselves as leg men will notice. If you really want to stand out, consider your swing plane.

Golf schools teach that it is a fundamental rule of good golf that your club follow a certain circular path throughout the swing. A good swing plane will get you more than a good shot; it also will garner you a big compliment from your pro. A classic golf swing, however, carries little clout on the golf course.

If you do not believe me, then go ahead. Borrow against your 401(K) plan to pay for the 3,894 lessons it takes to develop a perfect classical golf swing. Then guess what the other members in your foursome will say behind your back.

"She really has a good swing. She took tons of lessons. Just goes to show you need no natural talent to get good in golf…just a whole lot of money."

However, if you reverse pivot, collapse your wrist, distort your swing, and still hit the ball seventy-five yards, what a different reaction you will get!

"I just don't know how she manages to spin that club out of that S-shaped path in time to actually hit the ball!" one golfer marvels to the other after watching you in motion.

"That's nothing," he responds. "Did you see her on the last hole? She bowed her right leg down, pulled her left arm up during her downswing, twitched her head around like an ostrich, and still managed to drive her ball 150 yards. I tell you, she could be a pro!"

A Woman's Guide to Making Every Three-Foot Putt

Just as a man can, a woman can make every 3-foot putt. All you have to do is follow a few simple procedures.

First, get your ball on the green. USGA rules require that you hit it there. Men may direct you to "pick up your ball and throw it on the green." They will recommend this when they are concerned that you may slow things down; that is, they will recommend this anytime they are playing with or behind you. If they don't play this way, neither should you. *Hit* your ball up there.

Your next step is to evaluate the lie of your ball in relation to the hole. To do this, approach the ball from behind and carefully eyeball the lay of the green. Walk around the green; read every blade of grass rash enough to have grown between your ball and the hole.

If the area between your ball and the hole is flat, carefully brush off any real or imaginary sediments that may have settled between your ball and its proper home. Then place your putter in front of your ball and visualize the stroke that would send that ball rolling into its underground condominium.

Once you have visualized success from a place where your ball is *not* located, place your putter behind your ball and practice a few backstrokes, visualizing success from where it *is* located.

If you are right-handed, keep your right eye over your ball, your left hand dominant, and your wrists rigid. Left-handers will use the opposite eye and hand positions, but the wrist instruction applies to everyone.

If anyone speaks during any part of this visualization exercise, give that person a dirty look and start the procedures all over again. Pretty soon the people playing golf with you will become bored with your hesitancy. They will begin to look around. If you are playing with men, they really will want to tell you to hurry up, but they won't. After all, they already told you to throw your ball on the green and you ignored them then. If you keep playing your game the way you want to, after they told you what they want, they think they'll start to look bad.

Thus, the members of your foursome will look behind you to see if the players in the rear are advancing. They will look toward the next tee box and wish they were there. They will, in short, start to look everyplace except at you. They are getting angry with you, and they do not want to let you think that, at this point, they have any interest in your ball whatsoever.

You are now ready to putt. Draw your putter back and slightly, ever so slightly, use it to push your ball. If necessary, keep that pushing motion in progress—a long, long putting stroke that never breaks contact with the ball—until the ball falls into the hole.

This system is only one-hundred-percent successful when the area between your ball and the hole is one-hundred-percent flat. If the area between your ball and the hole is not flat, you will need to follow the steps below instead.

Place the head of your putter in the hole; extend your arm, holding the shaft of the putter out so that it comes someplace over the vicinity of your ball. Open your mouth slightly; twist your tongue; vibrate your voice box; flex your jaw muscles, and coordinate all related muscles. Then pronounce with perfect diction, "Gimme."

Pick up your ball, toss it in the air once casually, and place it confidently in your pocket.

By following these proven principles, women golfers can putt just as well as men do.

Swing Thoughts of Men and Women Golfers

Remember when it used to be a compliment for a man to tell a woman that she thought like a man? How would that apply on the golf course? A woman walks up to the tee box, puts her ball down on a tee, stands in an approach, and thinks out loud. "I'll just smack the bejesus out of this bugger." She does. Her ball flies out of bounds into the woods. So what does the man she is playing with say about her? "Wow, she not only thinks like a man, she plays like one!"

Every good golfer has a successful swing thought. A good swing thought, however, should keep the golfer, or at least her ball, on course. "Thinking like a man" is not the path of the exceptional golfer. "Thinking like an exceptional golfer" is.

In essence, the experts agree. Prior to swinging, a golfer should concentrate on her swing—not on the ball itself. There are a couple of reasons for this.

First, a golfer can always yell at her ball to grow legs, bite, stay up, or run after she hits it. During her ball's takeoff, however, she, rather than her ball, should be in command.

Second, there is a direct (or at least indirect) correlation between the direction, distance, and speed of the ball with the path and speed of the golf club as it swings toward the ball. Unfortunately, however, while it may be accepted practice for golfers to talk to their golf balls, if a golfer talks to her clubs instead, somebody is going to call the women with white coats.

"Go ahead and hit that ball squarely," Sally instructs her driver.

She must be nuts, her cart mate, Sue, thinks. Sue gets out of their cart and hits her ball. Next she screams wildly after it, "Run, run!" Next she surreptitiously pulls out her cellular phone and dials 911. "We have a live wire here on the sixteenth hole," she whispers. "I am playing golf with a woman who is talking to her golf clubs."

The good woman golfer, of course, avoids this scenario. She does not want to be escorted off the course. She thus talks to herself about how she is going to hit her clubs and never speaks aloud to any inanimate object except her ball. Furthermore, she knows that if she keeps concentrating on her swing, pretty soon it will look so good that it will not matter if her balls slice or hook ninety degrees. No one in her foursome—not even a man!—will know why. Now that would make her truly exceptional.

A woman golfer usually takes this piece of advice as she does medicine. A man may be unwilling to take an aspirin, but a woman is perfectly willing to overdose on any potential cure.

Once a woman golfer finds out how a swing thought could help her game, she quickly makes the transition from thought requirement to mandatory internal dialogue. Let's see. Keep my head down; my left arm stiff; my right arm flexible. Pretend I'm swishing a bucket back and forth. No! No! I'll pretend I'm sweeping with a broom. Okay. Don't forget to keep sitting on that imaginary bar stool while shifting my weight. Heels down. (Why, it's almost like horseback riding.) All right, now get serious. Act natural. Kiss that baby goodbye!

The last part of the average woman's swing thought will be the typical man's single thought. One approach really is no better than the other. Well, unless you want your ball to end up on *your* fairway.

Why Men Waggle More Than Women Wiggle Their Clubs

Ever notice what a man does when he gets on the tee box, and he is about to take his turn to drive? The first thing he does is he doesn't. He doesn't drive, that is. Like a young boy with a new bat, the man golfer about to drive spends a lot more time in the "about" stage than in the "drive" part.

The man who is up walks over to his teeing ground and surveys the hole. Sure, he was standing on that same tee box while his three buddies hit their drives. When he was standing there then, though, he was watching their balls, looking for possible sky hooks or out-of-bounds slices. He forgot that their balls end up in the fairway, and that is why his turn has been dead last for the past fourteen holes.

Now it is his turn, and he surveys the hole on his time. He looks for his opponents' balls. OK, OK, he saw them before, but then he was looking at them so he could tell everyone he saw where they went. He is looking at them now to determine if he can outdrive them.

After all, even if he cannot, he is not wasting time. He also uses this time to figure out what he will say if his ball is short. Maybe he'll explain why he prefers his second shot to be a 150-yard 5-iron rather than a 90-yard wedge. Maybe he'll tell them something about his aching back.

Thinking of his back, he decides to stretch out just a little bit. His muscles get so cramped in a golf cart. He may not have the energy to do the macarena on a Saturday night, but he is willing to put a yoga instructor to shame on the tee box. He rotates his arms back and forth, back and forth, with his club behind his back. He looks like an out-of-work actor trying out for the role of some tormented soul in a horror flick.

Enough of that. He grabs a tee, puts his ball on it, and plunges it into the earth. He is ready, ready, ready. He is ready, that is, to begin his waggle.

All men waggle. Their waggles vary considerably. Some men prefer to take their clubs back four or five times, three inches to three feet. Others take their clubs back progressively more distance every time they waggle. A few men don't bring their clubs back at all. They move them perpendicular to their stance instead. "Bring the club up and back—not just back," they remind themselves.

Most men waggle from three to thirty-three times. This man

waggles five or six times, a few inches each time. He is now ready to proceed. He is going to hit his ball, take a practice shot, or begin waggling again.

He asks himself how he feels. Feel really counts at this moment. He believes this because, like all men, he believes his waggles hold the magical power of flight. Like a witch's broomstick, clubs need to be enchanted to act enchantingly.

We women do not waggle. We women do not spend an inordinate amount of time on the tee box getting ready to hit. We women all make the same mistake. We do not rely on the power of the waggle. We put our faith in just dumb skill.

Did you ever notice how fascinating a man's waggle is? A man with a good waggle is like a man with a good cigar. He may stink, but at least he looks impressive.

Every golfer knows impressions are worth something. That is why we keep taking lessons even though we do not play any better after them. Pros sometimes even teach men the art of waggling. They believe these one-quarter swings grab the golfer's attention. The golfer will thus focus on his takeaway, visualize success in his swing, and, more important, silence his doubts within.

The waggles do work—sort of. The male golfer gets up and chops away at the air. After three or four of these semipractice backswings, he looks up. Yup, the course is still there. A couple of more swipes. Yup, these waggles sure build confidence! He hasn't missed the air once.

Okay, I want this ball to land right about there, he thinks as he lines up to the course once again. He nails it. His ball heads out. "This had better be a good one," he says. He was, after all, ready. He waggled.

Contrast this with the way a woman approaches the tee box. She wants to get on and get off as fast as possible. She does not like to stand on the tee box and wonder what to do and how to do it. She knows what to do. Rip and roar! Practicing twelve-inch introductions only makes the game more pressured and less pleasurable for her. She thus takes a quick overview of the hole while her friends are teeing off. Then it is her turn. Bang! She spanks her ball and it flies.

We women are fast off the tee box but slow in professionalism. Whoever saw a professional golfer hit a ball without going through the mental discipline of rehearsing the swing first? Wiggling may have gone out of style, but waggling has not. Men golfers look like pros when they are on their tees; we, on the other hand, look like slouches when we jump up to bat.

We need to put on our armor of collared T-shirts. We need to go out there and wage war against our waggleless women's world. Men cannot create this change for us. We have to do it for ourselves. The results would be phenomenal. In fact, if men had to wait for us a little longer on the tee box, they would stop saying we played slowly. They would be too busy watching our waggles and looking for our balls.

Play Smart, Swing Less: A Woman's Guide
to Course Management

Smart golfers hit the high-percentage shots. Everyone knows that. The problem is, however, most golfers do not want to play smart. They want to play well.

Most golfers, for instance, would probably score much better hitting higher lofted clubs—even their irons—from the tee box than they would using their driver. Take your 5-wood out of your bag to tee off on a par-five, however, and you won't feel good or smart. No one will think you are, either. They will, in fact, have another name for you—a beginner.

What do you aim for when you are in a sand trap that has a brim taller than you are bordering the green, but an easy out onto the fairway? Pretty silly question, isn't it? If you are like most golfers, you know it would be crazy to aim for the flag. Why, you can't even see it because that brim is so tall! That would be a really stupid move. No, no way will you line up for the flag; instead you line up to hit your friends on the green. "Heads up!" you yell, hoping their stretching necks will give you the one or two extra inches you need to have a really good target.

What about when you are faced with the "lay up" versus the "go for it" decision? Maybe you must accomplish either a 160-yard carry with a deadstop ball, or you can hit a 60-yard punch and then a one-hundred-yard carry. The smart golfer asks herself how far she usually hits; the average golfer asks her friends what they intend to hit. The good golfer? Why, she lets it rip. At least, this is how we think until score compilation.

The trick is always to get your ball in a lie where it will not only be advantageous to play smart, but also where it would be stupid to do otherwise. For instance, if you drive your ball 300 yards on a par-5 from the red tees, you will not have to worry about whether you should choose an iron versus a fairway wood for your second shot. Likewise, if your ball does not end up in the tall grass, you will not have the dilemma of deciding whether you should hit an 8-iron versus a 3-wood to get out of it. This just proves you do not have to be smart to get low scores. You can be a very good golfer and come out ahead, too.

Of course, winning involves more than playing your ball; it also requires you to consider how your opponent is playing his or her game. Say, for instance, you are playing against another woman. Your game is a match-play format. Your ball is behind a tree and one hundred yards behind hers, which is sitting on the side of the green. You have already taken one stroke more than she has. So you go for it. It's not a high percentage shot, but it is a smart way to play.

Now let's assume that your ball is on the green and twenty feet from the hole. Your opponent's ball is behind the tree. By some miracle, when she hits that ball, it dodges the branches and winds up on the green four feet from the hole. It's your turn to putt.

Should you go for it? If you make your putt, you will beat her on that hole. Should you lag putt and hope to tie her instead?

Well, again, if you want to play smart, you must consider your competition. If your opponent is a woman, you have to ask yourself, "Is she a good putter? Does she putt well under stress?" If you have a male opponent, on the other hand, only your putting matters. It will be a gimme for him anyway.

In the tournaments between the sexes, there are also other strategies to keep in mind. For instance, all men choose to use the club that has the highest percentage of success in a pro's hands. A man's idea of smart club selection is choosing between Callaway and Cobra. Women, on the other hand, usually put a lot of thought into club selection even on the course. This is especially true after they have mishit a ball.

"I knew it! I knew I had the wrong club the minute I picked it up. I should have used a 7-wood," shouts the woman who just lost her ball in the woods after scooping it out of the sand with a wedge.

Men golfers play smart by choosing good partners. "He only has a 3 handicap. Let's invite him!" the man says to the other two members of what is to be a four-person scramble team. Women golfers play smart by being truthful about their handicaps. "So what if we only get one-quarter of our combined handicaps? We can probably break a 108 in a scramble if we are playing really well, anyway."

All men prefer to hit their balls over water rather than laying up. Their idea of playing smart is forgoing the extra stroke that a layup takes. Women who lay up get condescending looks from men who do not. "Good idea, smart play," he says to his woman opponent as he walks over to his ball to attempt a 260-yard carry from the dirt where his ball lies.

Men think women play smart because they can't play well. Women think they play well because they play smart. It all comes back to those age-old questions...the chicken or the egg...the match or the mulligan.

Sweet Swing Sounds

Men and women golfers hear a very different game. The first thing a man hears on the tee box is his neck cracking as he stretches into golfer shape every way possible. He then approaches his ball. He backs off and takes one or two practice shots. Whoosh! Whoosh!

He waggles; sometimes grass stirs as he mistakenly makes a divot. Then he takes that backswing all the way back, one downward stroke. Whoosh! The ball punches holes in the sky.

Watchful eyes follow the ball and then there is silence—silence interrupted only by his shout to the golfers in the adjoining fairway, "Fore!"

Women golfers might forgive themselves, as men do, the need to yell "Fore!" if only they could make that "whoosh" noise. Contrary to popular opinion, that whoosh noise does not come from the speed of the swing. After all, even beginning men golfers can whoosh their balls. No, there is a scientific explanation for that whoosh noise. The noise arises from the vacuum of air that accumulates where breasts appear in a woman's swing path.

Not only is this my opinion, but I have heard pros express that same thought. Now, ladies, they may not come right out and say this. Yet how many of us have heard a man pro say, "Put your arms out a little more, hang them naturally—like an ape." You might think, "Gee, thanks—natural like an ape." Recognize, though, that he is concerned with the elimination of any obstruction (your chest) from your swing path. A larger-chested friend of mine once told me that a female pro advised her, "Don't try to move your arms around your breasts. Just hold your arms down naturally (like a woman)." She was happy with that.

I keep waiting for some advice with which I might be happy. If only, if only, some male pro looked worried about my "arm placement," I might consider saving up for a new set of clubs instead of breast implants.

Despite the petite size of my breasts, however, I still don't hear that whoosh noise. A woman golfer's swing just sounds different from a man's. For instance, women click their balls instead of their necks. It's a good solid click: the quality sound that breaks the silence when you hit the sweet spot! Now that's a sound that keeps bringing you back!

Women also hear the plop—that aural vacuum of space that

turns on sound waves when the ball rolls into the hole. It's a beautiful sound—far superior to the rustle of a pocket that men hear when they pick up their ball six feet short of the hole and drop it in.

Staying in Rhythm in the Face of Slow Play

We all know that feeling. You have a group of golfers in front of you, probably male, who keep holding you up. You don't want to lose the rhythm of the game. What can you do to stay in the zone when you have to take your club out of action?

Do what men golfers do when you are on the first tee box, just getting ready to begin your game. Stretch your swing a little bit. Hit three or four practice shots as fast as you can. Then put your left hand on your left hip. Spread your legs apart. Grasp a long iron with your right hand. Lean your body into your right hand and extend the club you are holding into the ground.

Finally, open your eyes wide; grimace with your lips and cheeks; practice a long stare of disdain. Keep the rhythm this way and you will prove that you can play the moment just as well as any of the boys can.

Fourth Hole

The Woman Golfer's Shopping Guide

The Pro Shop

The golf industry in the United States is estimated to bring in $15 to $20 billion per year. That's a lot of green.

Statistics show that the average man golfer plays about nineteen times a year, at a cost of $617, while the average woman golfer plays about fourteen times a year, at a cost of $452. Interestingly, however, almost *half* of all women golfers claim they have a "high interest" in the game. These same women play roughly twenty-seven times a year, at a cost of about $800. In addition, women golfers make up only about 20 percent of all golfers but, with the exception of clubs, they buy 50 percent of all golf products,

The presence of women in golf is growing dramatically. Only

5.4 million women play golf in the United States today, but more than half of all golfers who are trying golf for the first time are women. Thus, looking at golf from a marketing perspective, women are not only spending one big pile of money on the game, they are also about to spend a whole lot more.

Rest assured, however, that the money will not make its way into the ordinary pro shop. After all, the ordinary pro shop does not cater to statistics; it caters to men. In fact, ladies, if you look around at all of the ladies' golf equipment and wares available at the ordinary pro shop, your head will have to turn an arc of only about 10 degrees. The other 350 degrees will be filled with visions of men stuff. This not only conveys the impression ever so slightly that men are more welcome than women on the course, it also gives men the decided advantage in loosening up their neck muscles before they begin to play.

"Why don't you stock more women's merchandise?" you ask the clerk.

"Men golfers buy more merchandise in the shop than female golfers. The stuff in the women's section just doesn't move," he explains.

Ladies, why do you think that is? Do you think it has something to do with the fact that the pro shop carries women's clothing only in sizes 4 and 6 ? Or do you think it is because women just do not like to shop?

Choosing Golf Equipment

Ben Franklin was wrong. There is more certainty in life than just death and taxes. There is also the very reliable need for "just one more" piece of golf equipment.

"If only," you say, "I had an Alien wedge (or a Titanium Cobra driver or a Bubble Burner 7-wood or a Ping putter). Then I would have everything I need."

You are absolutely right. You would—until there was an advancement in state-of-the-art golf equipment or until someone in your foursome picked up a new club. As soon as that happened, of course, you would need just one more piece of equipment.

There is a very simple reason we golfers need to keep buying equipment. The stuff we own doesn't work. Take the typical metal woods. Maybe you paid $200 a club for these last year. Yet metal woods are like old-fashioned lawnmowers. You have to push like heck to get any work out of them. Buy titanium, however, and now you have space-age technology. Heck, if that stuff is good enough to get a rocket into space, it ought to at least get your ball an extra two yards down the fairway. Sure, it might cost a little. What are you working your butt off for, though? Your mortgage or your golf expenses?

Now consider your wedges. You used to carry two wedges—a pitching wedge and a sand wedge. Then someone in your foursome started carrying a lob wedge. She could do things with that which you never could do with your two outdated clubs. Sure, sure, she could do things with other clubs you could not do either. She has a great short game. Yet if someone with a great short game needs that club, shouldn't you consider getting one?

So you start looking around. Lo and behold, the question is not whether you should update your set with a lob wedge. The question is whether you should toss out your lousy clubs and buy an entire collection of wedges.

Golfers can buy a wedge to cover every possible distance except the empty space ear to ear. It is easy to fill that space in with questions, though. How would I play with a bag filled with twelve wedges, one driver, and a putter? Or what about twelve wedges, one putter, and a 3-wood? Will I even need a putter, though, if I have twelve wedges?

It is enough to drive you crazy—or at least out golfing. Maybe we women just should be honest with ourselves. We talk golf as if we know it all. We do not. We even buy the wrong clubs because we do not know the right ones to buy. You know what I mean by the right ones—the ones that will give you 260-yard drives every time you drive and which will ensure you birdie every hole.

You should not be too harsh on yourself, though. It is tough to get information on golf equipment. You can read golf magazines, of course, but reading about golf equipment is like reading a green. Everyone does it but it doesn't do anyone a bit of good. You are about as likely to pick out the equipment that is best for you from reading a magazine as you are to get a hole in one on a par-4 from the blue tees. It is, in short, not in your game today.

Women golfers in search of equipment thus must rely on the store clerks and owners who sell that equipment. Walk into the typical golf store and tell the first clerk you see that you want to buy some golf equipment.

"For you or someone else?" he asks.

Now, when a man goes into a store to buy a new set of sticks, no one asks him if he is looking for something for his wife. He is directed to the men's club section first and asked questions later. Much later.

The first thing the clerk will say to the man is, "Assume your golf position." Then he will pull out a tape measure and start measuring the distance between the man's wrists and the floor when the man is in his best golf pose. The man, of course, will assume this pose while looking into a mirror. It is an ideal approach posture. It looks great. In fact, his posture is so good he never will be able to assume it again, unless of course he happens to play on a course that posts mirrors at the tee boxes. Men are fitted to clubs. They are fitted to clubs that do not fit, but *would* fit if each man were a really good player or carried a six-foot portable mirror in his golf bag.

In contrast, women who shop at the average golf shop never have a problem with a club fitting. Since all women are the same height and weight, all they need to do is look for clubs with the engraved letter *L*. *L* is the universal symbol for ladies'. One size fits all.

Well, it does for everyone except those show-offs. Those tall women. Tall women always purchase senior men's clubs. They always get a lot of those clubs to choose from, too. After all, few senior men buy senior clubs. Senior men stand so tall and strong when they are fitted for clubs that the men's senior clubs never fit them in the pro shop. Senior clubs fit only tall women and senior men who are actually playing.

In any event, for the woman golfer, size is not a factor in the golf-equipment decision. The only exceptions are those women who shop in women-friendly golf stores. The store representatives in these shops worry about things like fit, swing speed, and other complicated stuff reserved for men in other stores. Women-friendly pro shops do not sell clubs as one-size-fits-all. Rather, one store can fit all sizes. In other words, they fit women as they do men. Fortunately for women, they still can get clubs that fit. This is because women are much more used to looking in mirrors, and thus it does not affect their stance during the fitting.

Regardless of where you shop and how you are fitted, however, you eventually have to take some swings and make some decisions as to which clubs swing best. Women select golf clubs on the same basis that they discard them. They choose them on performance.

The average woman golfer decides to discard her clubs based

on her own performance. She buys her clubs, however, based on someone else's. Maybe she will consider what clubs are used by her favorite professional golfer, or the best woman golfer in her league, or a stranger she got paired up with last week.

If we want to have our equipment work for us, however, we are going to have to consider our own games instead. We must realize we are individuals. The women we imitate are outstanding golfers; most of us are not. It stands to reason, then, that the only way we are ever going to get good is to play with bad golfers' clubs. Make that the ladies' version.

The Size of a Man's Clubs Does Not Predict Much of Anything

What woman would ever look at an oversized putter and say, "I know. Let's call it a Hog"? OK, maybe some motorcycle mama might. The average woman golfer, however, would not come up with that name.

What woman would view forgiveness the way the Killer Bee marketers do? They say this club, with its "bullwhip" shaft, is forgiving. It's so forgiving that, when you hit it, it's like a bullwhip. Silly me. When I think of a bull there are other attributes which dirty, I mean drive, my mind. I have never even thought of the forgiving bullwhip.

What did you think of when you heard the name Big Bertha

the first time? Did you think of a voluptuous cartoon character? Or a lady of the night? Or a graphite shaft with a head on the end?

These golf club names all have something in common. They make money. Men golfers like to buy products that make them feel big, important, and exciting. Men like products with names that make golf sound as if only men should play. Men want to feel that when they play golf they are involved in some rough-and-tumble adventure. "Better leave the ladies at home. No way could they possibly be up to this!"

Men want to create this perception because they don't want to face the truth. Athletic men play football and baseball. Daring men race cars and durable men ski. Aerobically fit men jog and play tennis. Adventurous men fly planes and sail seas. Outdoors men go on safaris and white-water rafting trips. Spiritual men fly-fish and fire-walk. What do the remaining men do? They golf.

Timid men have a real attraction to golf. Unlike football, soccer, or boxing, you cannot get hurt playing golf. Oh, sure, there are the occasional cuts from sharp pieces of grass, the back sprains from bad swings, the broken arms from grabbing your beer when your golf cart is moving, and the tragic errant-ball incidents. A golfer can get his shoes wet in a water hazard or get a sunburn in the sand, but overall the biggest pain a golfer will ever incur from the sport is to his or her ego. Men avoid that exposure, at least to some extent. They avoid playing with women. That way, at least they won't lose to them, by golly.

This does not mean that golf is not a demanding avocation. Golfers need strong technical knowledge. They have to learn a fancy credit and debit system. They have to know how to read golf maps and how to pretend to know how to read greens. Men who golf have to be bilingual. Here in the United States, for instance, they must speak English and betting. Men golfers also must have some athletic ability. If a male golfer wants to play on a level with his peers, he should be able to kick a bad ball out of the woods and a good ball into a perfect lie without losing his balance or otherwise drawing undue attention to himself. In short, while golfing does require a lot of skills, it does not require the physical prowess, courageous outlook, and devil-may-care attitude that a fighter pilot needs.

Men golfers, however, are willing to pay plenty to make their game sound a little more manly than croquet. They want clubs with names that make them sound rough and ready. They also want big clubs. The average male golfer wants to hit oversized golf heads, overly long woods, and shoulder-height putters. His idea of fit is *Big*. After all, he will reason, you get a lot more speed out of long shafts, a lot more power behind big heads, and a lot more gimmes with long putters.

Like the cavemen of old, men on the course wave their clubs around like symbols of strength. Faced with tough tee shots, men golfers waggle their drivers as if they were summoning the spirits of old to make their kills swift and plentiful. It just would not be the same with some club advertised as a "fairy godmother wand." Men like clubs with macho names. For instance, after that most humiliating moment in golf—a whiff—what man wants to toss some lightweight-named club around? Better to dramatically clobber a Killer Bee into the ground with a look of disgust than to sling around some club called the Long-Stemmed Pansy.

It's OK for these marketers to humor men with some marketing hype. It's OK, even though we women often are stuck playing with clubs that have those same funny names. After all, if our clubs had different names, it might get confusing.

Can't you just see the confusion? You'd be shopping at your local pro shop. Once again the clerk would be trying to sell you equipment for your husband. "No, no, no," you would irritably respond. "How many times do I have to tell you? I don't want a Big Bertha. I want a Big Dick."

Looking Good on the Course

Looking good on the golf course comes as naturally to us women golfers as it does to Miss America contestants. In other words, we have to work hard at it. It takes more than sweat and training to transform a woman standing in a fairway or on a runway into a knockout (or at least a knockoff) beauty. It takes money.

The golf fashion industry rakes in more bucks than we rake bunkers. The National Golf Foundation estimates $775 million is spent in the United States each year on golf attire. That does not leave us much money to buy lipstick.

Thus, unlike beauty contestants, we women golfers are light on our use of cosmetics. We have more elements to worry about than runway lights anyway. We encounter wind, sand, sun, humidity, sand, sweat, rocks kicked up by our golf carts, sand, water, sand, and sand. We therefore do not bother putting on three layers of foundation to look natural, as a contestant might. We just slip on some 45 + SPF sunscreen, a little bit of gloss, and that waterproof mascara which streaks rather than runs. The heck with foundation, powder, and the other works. Why should we concern ourselves with color? We will be in the shade the whole afternoon anyway. By this, I do not mean we will be hitting our balls out of the woods all afternoon. Only men golfers do that. We women find our shade elsewhere—under our visors and hats.

There are all kinds of golfing hats.

- There are slick souvenir visors that cost twenty dollars each and sport the names of courses that cost two to ten times that amount to play.
- There are fancy Texas hats which give a whole new twist to the Texas two-step. Let's see... It's backswing and throughswing ...backswing and throughswing.
- There are baseball caps. Athletic women like them.
- Then there are Fiesta hats. Country club women like them.

Fiesta hats come in all kinds of colors and have all kinds of bows, flowers, and designs on them. Shopping for a Fiesta hat is like buying an Easter bonnet. You are not looking for something just to cover your head. You want something that makes you look and feel good.

Few women skimp on cost when buying a golf hat. After all, once you put a golfing hat on, it stays there. All day. If you mistakenly take it off, you will remember why you keep it on. "Oh my God, will you look at my hair!" Lawyers, doctors, secretaries, and professors may have bad-hair days—except, that is, when they are on the golf course. Then they are golfers. Golfers, at worst, have old-hat days.

Women golfers have more in common than hats. We also all have class. There is, in fact, simply no such thing as a sloppy woman golfer. I guess all that training in bunkers equips us to groom ourselves well, too.

Women golfers like to dress for the links, and the fashion industry is only too happy to oblige. Tee-Wear, Lily's of Beverly Hills, Bette & Court, E. P. Pro, and Izod are just some of the brands from which we can choose today. Not only are golf brands all expensive. They also all have advertisements that show women golfers on a course looking absolutely great in their harmoniously mismatched attire. I hate those women. Those clothes look so natural on them. It's as if they were born wearing mix and clash. I, on the other hand, had the misfortune of growing up in a mix-and-match socioeconomic environment.

I can still remember my sister's voice. "Don't wear plaids and stripes together. They clash. Don't wear orange and red together. They clash. Avoid vests that have nothing in common with the rest of your outfit."

"Yeah, she's right. In fact, you should avoid vests, period," my best friend chimed in. "They're for bustier girls."

As a result of those strictures from my youth, today I cannot even open my closet and find the clothes that naturally mismatch, to comply to that eclectic "I'm too rich to worry about conforming" conformity. I have to look at the inside labels rather than the outward colors to figure out which of my shirts do not look as if they belong with the shorts with which they originally were sold as a set. "Let's see, what does this pink-, blue-, and white-toned vest mismatch? Hmmm...maybe the yellow shorts with the blue flags? Maybe the blue shorts with the orange golf balls?" I check the labels. "Oh, the black, blue, and white shorts with the black golf shirt. I should have guessed. The colors are so dissimilar."

Wearing outrageous clothes is just as much a part of golf as chasing that elusive white ball. Knickers may go in and out of style (right now, by the way, they are in) but clash is a golfing staple.

I thus have become like other women. I may be a closet conformist but no one can tell from looking at me that my natural tendency is to wear a beige shirt with beige shorts or a red, white, and blue shirt with blue shorts. That tendency is an easy one to hide. Even women with no golf fashion sense can look stylish on the course. All we have to do is what our friends with fashion sense do. Spend a few hundred dollars for an outfit in which to swing, sweat, and swear (very softly).

Pink Balls and Other Handicaps You Can Buy

When Sally Voss Krueger was playing in the AT&T Pebble Beach National Pro-Am, not all of the men watching the tournament were equally impressed by the fact that a woman was participating in the game. Some men actively cheered for her. Yet one of the spectators, obviously focusing more on her gender than her outstanding ability, reportedly questioned whether she was using a pink ball.

Obviously, very few golfers—men or women—will ever develop their skills to the level of someone like Sally Voss Krueger. Thus, golfers use another characteristic to measure each other. They assess your outlook—that is, how seriously you play.

The seriousness, as distinct from the skill, of a player is considered extremely important. After all, golf is a game to golfers only when they have just lost very, very badly. At all other times it is a religion to be practiced in Saturday service with the respect, awe, and thankfulness of any other life creed. Tithes to the golfing manufacturer can reap considerable grace and goodwill on the golf course—at least before you begin playing. Thousand-dollar clubs may not improve a golfer's game, but at least they reflect some dedication to it.

The golf-seriousness assessment of a newly assigned partner begins before the first tee. "What kind of clubs do you have there?" the golfer asks his newly assigned male partner.

"Ping" is the proud reply.

Must be a good golfer! the first man thinks.

When that same man gets paired up with a woman who carries pink balls, a golf-stroke-calculator bracelet, cheap clubs, and a Sunday bag on eighteen holes, he is likely to think, Looks as if she'll be playing golfer instead of golf.

Women are not wanna-be golfers. They thus should not carry equipment that creates a light-headed, 40-handicap image.

Serious women golfers know this. They do not use pink balls. They use classic white balls or they use those ugly orange balls that men with poor vision and poorer taste sometimes use. They use pink balls only when they are playing with men who gave them pink balls as a present and when they do not want to hurt the men's feelings by not using their gift.

Of course, ball manufacturers keep making pink balls, even though women don't buy them. That's because men keep buying them for women. Women can stop this gift-selection process pretty quickly, however. All they have to do is reciprocate any gift of pink balls with a gift of blue balls. All men avoid blue balls.

Never think that the outcome of the game is determined by balls alone, though. Serious women golfers do not color-coordinate their golfing attire, golf bag, and golf clubs. A department store's mix and match also indicates a wanna-be.

Golfers size up each other's seriousness quotient pretty quickly, and they never let actual performance impact their evaluation. After all, even good golfers have bad days and even bad golfers get lucky.

What you play with, how you look using what you play with, and how you talk about how you play determines your golfing social handicap. Golfers use these factors to assess the people they play with, because they are fair and objective people. As such, they prefer to use real numbers, such as the cost of clubs—rather than imaginary numbers, such as a golfer's handicap—to determine who dabbles in, rather than plays, the game of golf.

All I Want for Christmas Is...

Due to the poor shopping conditions for women shoppers at many pro and discount golf shops, stores for women golfers are becoming quite popular. The storekeepers in such places really cater to their female clientele. In fact, at least one of these stores has introduced a novel idea for women who love golf and the men who love them. In that store, a woman can make a list of golfing supplies she wants for Christmas, and then her significant other can stop by and shop from that list.

Here's a sneak preview, for my secret Santa, of my wish list for the upcoming golf season:

- a driver as expensive as his
- a par score on my regular course
- a handicap less than my age
- the right to play golf on Saturday anywhere I can afford to play golf on Saturday
- the ability to worry about *my* game when I am playing with him and *his* game is off
- the right to use my pull cart on any course I play
- the need to put my driver away and select another club so I can lay up 220 yards from the red tees

Fat-Footed Women

Fat-footed women can't play golf. Golf instruction books try to put a positive spin on physical differences. Left-handers may whine about discrimination after they shoot a 140, but they can buy books that give reversed instruction. There is also plenty of literature as to how short, muscular people should take advantage of their upper-body strength and how tall, thin people should utilize their wider swing arc.

Ask yourself, however, when did you last read golfing tips for fat-footed women? Let's face it, you have never seen tips for fat-footed women. This is because they really cannot play the game. It would be like writing a golf instruction book for cats or dogs—pretty useless, even though they may like chasing after little white balls.

Golf discount stores recognize this. Visit one of these stores and take a good look around. You'll see men's golfing shoes available from sizes Wimp Foot A to Bigfoot Double Wide. Then look at the women's golf-shoe collection. The width stops at the letter *B*.

Shoe manufacturers realize that fat-footed women can't play. They figure these women would probably slow the golf courses down so much that, if many of them did play, people with normal-size feet would give up the sport. That would be bad for their business. They thus restrict the pool of footgear for fat-footed females.

As a result, the only fat-footed women who can find golf shoes are those with fat feet and very, very fat wallets. Fat-footed shoes are available only in expensive golf stores. Despite the size of the product, there are no economies of scale here. Those fat-footed shoes are available only at the price a fat-footed man might pay for his Big Bertha club.

So Big (Footed) Bertha can't afford Big Bertha clubs. She plays in top-of-the-line $400 shoes with $79 clubs, while fat-footed men play in $79 shoes with $400 top-of-the-line drivers.

Yet a fat-footed woman won't admit she can't play. No, no. She goes out on the course and pretends she belongs there. Then, at night, she dreams of better clubs, Saturday-morning tee times, and fat shoes at a thin price.

Fifth Hole

Things to Talk About on the Golf Course

Changing Courses: Making Golf Your Career

Everyone dreams of making a hole in one. Yet that may not be what you consider when you are waiting for the foursome in front of you to finish their putts on a par-4 hole. You may have your sights on an even bigger miracle. You may be fantasizing about a job that would actually pay you to be on the golf course.

It may seem hopeless. You don't have a minus-2 handicap. You don't have a degree in greens management. In fact, you haven't even been able to get the grass in your backyard to grow back since you put in that practice bunker last year. (Furthermore, it was a major oversight to fail to consider that all the cats in your neighborhood would find that sand very attractive.)

Don't give up, though. There are plenty of job opportunities that could turn your dream into reality. All you need is a little imagination.

Opening a Research Consultant Agency

Corporations and associations spend a lot of money studying the impact golf has on women's lives. They have conducted all kinds of studies. There are, for instance, studies that show that

- a woman's income is inversely related to her handicap
- the average woman golfer has a household income of $55,000 per year and lives in a home that she owns
- a woman executive whose handicap is 10 or less earns about $140,000 per year
- a woman executive duffer earns about $100,000 per year
- successful women use golf as a business tool

You can create an excellent golfing career out of studies such as these. Obviously, the companies and associations that sponsored these studies wanted to have credible data. Yet their surveys are flawed. How are they flawed?

That's where your imagination comes in. You have to review the studies carefully to determine where the examiners used a research tool that you believe is not as reliable as it should be. For instance, most studies trust the information provided by the subjects. Do you know what that means? These guys actually believed these women when they reported their handicaps! Sure, sure, statistics don't lie. But golfers? Even women golfers occasionally miscount.

You want a job where you are paid to golf? Then get a company to sponsor your efforts in a legitimate study. Perhaps you might offer to do a study in which a company pays for all of your greens fees for a year, after which you report back what you did with the money you saved. Or perhaps you might offer to do a study in which you golf with other women and keep track of both their golf scores and their on-the-course business successes. The sponsoring company would not have to worry about your study affecting the other women's game or their business efforts. You would set up the study so that the women would think you were just coincidentally paired up with them.

It might, of course, raise some suspicion if you always showed up to play by yourself. You don't have to worry about getting an assistant, though. I'm free Saturday mornings.

Becoming a Sports Analyst

Being a golf analyst has to be a pretty nice job. Basically all a golf analyst does is watch golfers golf and talk about golf.

At first glance you may think there is not much difference between a professional golf analyst and your husband or boyfriend. After all, when your significant other watches golf on television, he explains to you why Tiger Woods made a mistake hitting that 385-yard drive. He, after all, would have played that hole just a little bit differently. There is a difference in the analyses, however. When professionals offer their "could have," "should have," "would have," observations, they are supposed to know what they are talking about—yet they do not. There is a real lack of talent in this field today. Golf analysts, in fact, have refused to even acknowledge the tough golf issues of today. This, of course, creates a real opportunity for *you*.

Consider the saga surrounding Ben Wright. Ben Wright was a golf analyst with CBS. He worked there from 1972 through 1996. Then, in January 1996, the president of CBS announced that Wright would not be a part of the broadcast team for CBS's first tournament of the season. He also said that CBS had no plans for Wright's return to CBS golf tournaments. Ben Wright was not fired. There were, however, some people not employed by CBS who were happy to see him leave.

This is because Wright was caught up in a controversy. Specifically, the *News Journal* in Wilmington, Delaware, said that Wright had reported that women golfers "are handicapped by having boobs" and that "lesbians in the sport hurt women's golf." Mr. Wright denied making the statements. The National Organization for Women, the Ladies Professional Golf Association, and the Gay and Lesbian Alliance Against Defamation were unhappy with Wright, however.

When faced with this news, how did other golf analysts react? Did they put their analytical skills to work and force the public to confront the tough issues? They could have joined together and said, "Okay, golfers, let's take a look at these important issues. It really does not matter whether Mr. Wright made these statements. The crucial issue is whether the things they said Wright said were right." They did not do any such thing. The golf analysts failed us.

You may yet thank those analysts for their oversight. They have left someone—maybe you—a great topic for golf analysis. Maybe you can make a few bucks while standing on a beautiful golf course.

What do you say? Are we women handicapped by having boobs? If so, how should we deal with this inequity? Should clubs be required to add three subdivisions to their red tees? Red A, Red B, and Red Jumbo? What about that occasional fat man who makes the slender woman jealous? Should he be able to advance his tee to match his size?

What about those lesbians? How should they be treated? If they are ruining the game for women, maybe we should require them to compete with men. I am sure men would feel much better knowing they may lose to a lesbian rather than to a heterosexual woman. After all, they may have already had that experience outside the game of golf. Yet if players were separated by sexual preference rather than by gender, would the performance for which the woman athlete would be judged be the one in which she was competing? Is the world ready for this concept?

Sure, sure, it sounds so simple. Yet it's not a solution without a problem. After all, you have to ask yourself: Once you resolve these issues, what else would you, the sports analyst, have left to analyze? Do you think men have any organs that also should be addressed?

Becoming a Country-Club Lawyer

Country-club law is also an industry that pays to put you on the green. Becoming a lawyer does not require nearly the commitment learning to golf does, either. It takes four years of college and three years of law school Try becoming a pro in the next seven years!

Of course, law is a lot like golf. Everyone can't be a professional. In fact, to become a lawyer you have to be really smart. Do you have the stuff to make the grade? Well, you do only if you are smart enough to pass this test.

Which do you find the most attractive area of practice?

- *a.* Silicone-breast litigation
- *b.* Tobacco defense
- *c.* Country-club law

Where do you think the most intelligent attorneys go to school?

a. Harvard
b. Yale
c. John Jacobs

If you answered *c* to both questions, you are smart enough to be a lawyer. Do you want to be, though? It could, after all, really interrupt your golf game. It's a tough decision, and only you can make it. The following information, however, may be helpful to your decision.

One of the primary responsibilities of a lawyer is the development of defense strategies. Thus, if a country club is sued for negligent course design because a member was hit by an errant ball, the country-club lawyer must figure out how to defend the country club. That requires a lot of investigation and discovery work.

Where will that work be done? On the course, of course. How the heck is a country-club lawyer going to prove course design had nothing to do with that accident unless she is familiar, really familiar, with the course layout? She is thus paid to plan her course—I mean trial—strategy. Country-club law is thus sort of like being a pro, except you can have a 30 handicap.

Taking a Mulligan May Prevent a Lawsuit

There are three sets of rules in golf. There are the formal "Rules of Golf." These are the rules professionals play by and amateurs play with. There are informal rules. We call these "golf etiquette." Golf etiquette is very important. It allows you to break the formal rules even when your competitor is looking. Then there are the rules of the unhappy golfer. These are the rules of litigation.

All golfers know the informal rules of golf and pretend to know the formal ones. Most, however, overlook the most authoritative rules—namely, the rules of litigation. This may be because even a cry of "Fore!" is more welcome on a golf course than the chant, "I'll sue!" You don't have to tell people you will sue them to get them to consider the authoritative rules, though.

For instance, next time your ball hits something that's not green, such as a cart path or a railroad track, and it gets a bad bounce, call the marshal over and demand that he authorize a mulligan. After he stops laughing, tell him about the case where a woman hit her ball into a railroad track and it boomeranged back and hit her right on the nose. She sued the golf course and won about $40,000. It was a good decision. After all, the course did not provide any warnings. No one had advised her that if she hit a ball onto the railroad tracks, it could ricochet back and cause her bodily injury.

Then say to the marshal, "Now, I do not want you to bend the rules just for me. Therefore, if you can show me a sign that states a bounce on that cart path could detour my ball and result in my financial loss, then I'll just play my ball where it lies. Otherwise, don't you think the course should either pay my lost bet or authorize my mulligan?"

Knowledge of litigation also comes in handy when your ball ends up in a poor lie on a fire-ant hill. Before you ask your opponent if you can move your ball, tell him about the lawsuit brought by a golfer who died after his ball landed in the very same place. This golfer, despite his partner's permission to pick up the ball, played it from the ant hill and got stung by some of the ants. When the golfer died soon afterward, his estate sued the golf course, claiming it was negligent in its pesticide treatment of mounds and that the golfer's cardiac arrest was caused by the stings. (The golf course claimed the tragic loss was caused instead by the golfer's obesity and smoking.)

Your opponent will not care that the jury found the defendant was not negligent, or that post-trial motions were filed. He will be too busy waving at you to pick up your ball and get the heck out of there.

Knowledge of the rules thus makes your round more enjoyable. Your score is not the only thing that benefits, however. You also benefit socially. Legal news makes great small talk when, for instance, your foursome is group number three waiting to tee off on a par-3.

Often golfers waiting around in these circumstances look around at the houses nearby until one of them is moved to comment, "Wouldn't it be just great to live on a course?" Next time, don't dumbly shake your head up and down like a vertical waggle on a man's swing. Don't smugly comment, "Well, actually, I already do." Instead, interest them with this piece of news. There have been lawsuits filed by people who bought houses on golf courses and then claimed their homes were devalued by all the golf balls that wound up in their yards.

Just don't let anyone get too absorbed as you discuss how you would decide this case if you were a judge or a jury member. After all, there also have been cases where golfers who have been hit with golf balls after someone yelled "Fore!" were found contributory negligent. Those golfers who were hit had failed to keep proper lookout. You don't want to be sued for contributing to anyone's improper lookout.

Litigation aside, safety is important, and the golf course is a very, very dangerous place to be. There are, after all, about 20 million men golfers out there.

Living on Course

To those people I golf with who say you can't buy happiness, I say, "Hah!" Buy a piece of golf-course property, and you buy yourself more than a prime piece of real estate. Real happiness, that's what golf-course property is all about.

Living on a golf course is living right. What do you actually get when you live on a course? A picturesque, parklike vista with someone else paying for the mowing, fertilizing, planting, and all of the other absolutely backbreaking labor necessary to give nature that natural look. The opportunity to jump over your fence and onto a fairway so that you can sneak in a hole or two while the steaks are on the grill. A neighborhood filled with your favorite kind of people—golfers. Finally, a chance to watch every type of golfer imaginable, up close and live, for free.

There is, in fact, an absolute joy that stirs inside when you wake up in a bedroom that overlooks your favorite golf course. In the summer, you see the dew on the grass, the sun as it rises, and a certain sand trap just waiting for your footprints. Maybe you could play hooky and hook the ball just this once. Let's face it, when you live on a golf course, pleasure is as much a part of your life as mulligans are part of your game.

People who don't live on golf courses have a hard time accepting this. They point to all of the empty pools in the backyards of fairway houses as they ride by on their rented golf carts. "Guess the residents are afraid to go out and use their pools," they muse to each other. "Must be concerned about errant balls." It is as if the people who live on the course are a bunch of dummies rather than duffers; it is as if these people intended to move to the beach but instead got confused and moved across from a sand trap.

Next time golfers say this to you, ask them why they think those people moved to the course in the first place. Any chance that they might like golfing more than swimming? Maybe the reason they are not in their pool is because they are out on the course.

Jealousy—that is what makes these nongolf-community dwellers think that way. They just can't stand it that someone else is living life better than they. You don't see jealousy among members of a planned community, however. No, sirree. No one who lives on a golf course worries if someone else's backyard is greener. They would not even notice it. Who would, with all of those white golf balls in everyone's backyard.

Live on a golf course and you will learn the joys of sharing. Trespassing signs nailed to your fence will keep your backyard as invasion free as handicaps keep golf tournaments fair. Live on a course and you will learn to count your blessings. You will rejoice in the occasional slicer who makes his way past your pool and into your garden to pick up a ball. Chances are he'll only claim one, and it will be the closest one to the fairway anyway.

Of course, life is not all play and no work. Even the hotshot golf-community dwellers occasionally have to worry about more than getting a triple bogey. They must, in fact, concern themselves with the business of making a living. It is a sad fact that no one likes to admit, but working is the only way most people can even afford their golfing habit.

One would think it would be easy for golfers to make the connections that would keep them in enough green to pay their greens fees. Even nongolfers hear the legendary tales of how golf leads to connections. Yet you will probably make good connections only if you belong to a high-class country club or live in a prestigious golfing community.

Living in a golf-course community enables you to mix with

the movers and shakers, as well as the slicers and hookers, in your area. Such communities obviously offer more than golf. The starter in such a club might put you in a foursome with someone who might invest in your business, someone else who might buy your products, and a 2 handicapper who will intimidate the heck out of your boss.

Old country clubs reek of old money and new opportunities. It helps to have a 4 handicap, but it helps even more to have $4,000 to shell out to play in a pro-amateur tournament.

Woman does not live on golf and bread alone, however. Golf course living provides certain social advantages as well. For instance, if you live on a southern golf course, you'll spend one night before Christmas each year as a caroler in a decked-out golf cart "sleigh" that is loaded with lights and hot rum toddies. If you live up north, you will spend an afternoon in February cross-country skiing with friends along the cart path that leads to the hole you aced last year.

Living on a golf course today is like living in the Wild West in days of old. It is romantic, it is adventuresome, and it can be lucrative. Indeed, it is the fulfillment of a lifetime dream of many senior citizens, the badge of honor of many corporate citizens, and the summer addiction of many people with old money.

People who live on a golf course have their lives on course. If only they could say the same thing about their golf balls... ahhh... then life would be really sweet.

Sixth Hole

Women Golfers Make the Best Friends

The Woman Golfer Friend

Women golfers make the best friends. A woman golfer does not get angry if you cannot attend her wedding or that of her daughter because of a previously scheduled golf outing.

She understands when you do not invite her to play golf on an absolutely perfect seventy-degree afternoon, with a tee time at the best course in town. She also acts thrilled when you call her at the very last minute and invite her to play, because one of your (and her) other best friends just backed out.

A woman golfer will tell you the name and phone number of the best pro who ever gave her lessons, so you will not waste your money on poor instruction elsewhere. She will not talk about you behind your back or throw undermining remarks your way as you hit the sticks.

A woman golfer is always positive. Hit a shot behind the green so that you now have to bypass a twenty-foot uphill bunker with a sand trap to get on the green, and she'll exclaim, "You can play that!" or "You really put some power in that shot!"

Chop your driver into the ground, leaving a three-foot divot, and a topped ball that wormburns 20 yards ahead, and she will say, "Just where you want it. Right down the fairway!" Hit a ball 125 yards up in the air. Watch it bounce into a tree, ricochet back and forth among branches, and fall in perfect line for an easy pitch to the green. She will smilingly affirm, "Planned that one right!"

Regardless of what tees she may usually play from, every woman golfer is a member of the "Red Tee Society." If she drives the ball 289 yards, and you drive the ball 89 yards, she will always choose to play the red tees when she is playing with you.

Women golfers play ready golf. A woman golfer is not hung up on honors or handicaps. All she wants to do is move quickly down the course—eighteen holes in roughly four hours and twenty minutes. She wants the two of you to avoid the most dreaded female stereotype—slow play. If that means you have to move your ball to an easy lie, or if you each have to pick up your ball at some point, the woman golfer is easy about it. Women golfers are the most considerate golfers on the golf course.

A woman golfer is also someone you can trust. Women golfers freely exchange intimacies, knowing that their secrets are as safe with their golfing friends as pink balls are from theft by male golfers.

"I think you're in the rough again."

A woman golfer reports her score truthfully (usually), yet she doesn't care if you do or not. She understands every golfer has his or her own perception of reality. If you choose to forgive yourself some minor or major misspent swing(s), she will not challenge you, unless it would be unfair to others because you are in a tournament or involved in a bet. A woman golfer accepts your score the way she accepts you—unconditionally.

Women golfers make the best friends. They tell you when they want you to be quiet, and they only ask your opinion when they want it. Women golfers don't criticize each other's game, husband, or philosophies. They bond with other women who love the game, and that love is enough to overcome lifestyle differences, socio-economic factors, and physical appearance.

Speaking of physical appearance, a woman golfer does not avoid female golfers who are more attractive, thinner, or younger than she is. She takes joy in her own body structure. Heavy women golfers complain about their weight but delight in the strength behind their drives. Thin women golfers may desire more curves but enjoy the agility of their swing. A woman golfer does not primp for a golfer class on video. She has more important things to consider: namely, her game.

Women golfers also never compete with each other for appreciative looks from male counterparts. Skeptics may say one of the reasons for this is they do not get them anyway. After all, men are too busy trying to avoid women on the course for women to worry about attracting them. The real reason for this, though, is that women golfers respect themselves and each other too much to worry about the attention of men on the golf course.

Women golfers make the best friends, which is good. For many women golfers, these are the only friends they have left by the end of the golfing season.

Other Athletes As Friends

Women golfers may make the best friends—but what about other sportswomen? Are they compatible companions for female golfers? Let's consider the evidence.

Tennis Players

Tennis players do not make the best friends for women golfers. Tennis players compete very aggressively with each other. They make it a point to yell out both their score and your score every time they serve. No golfer would shout at the end of the first hole, "Me par, Susan nine!"—yet tennis players think nothing of shouting out your losing score loudly enough so any passerby can learn how poorly you really play.

Tennis players like to play in cute little skirts and the color white. Their goal is to smash their ball at the farthest point possible from you, so you will run after it and then miss it—as if chasing after big yellow balls were an intelligent form of enjoyment.

Golfers don't require their friends to be aerobics worshipers. They also do not discriminate against the heavy gal who may not want to look like a melting marshmallow in pleats just to play a sport. Golfers help you find your ball; they don't purposefully try to make you lose it.

Unlike golfers, tennis players don't share intimacies. How intimate can you get when you are running around like crazy and the person you are playing with can't even keep something as simple as your score private? Golfers enjoy each other's company as they walk or ride to their balls.

Golfers also take delight in each other's successes and the beauty of the world around them. Tennis players do not appreciate nature. They usually play on clay, concrete, asphalt, or some other hard surface, on a rectangular area inside a chain-link fence.

Sad to say, tennis players are also very poor athletes—so poor that the rules of the game allow them to take a mulligan on every first shot. Nevertheless, they walk around like hotshots and pretend they are the only country-club members who get any exercise.

Aerobic Dancers

Women who take aerobics wear thongs as they compete for best-body award. Aerobics goers show up at a class, stake out unmarked territory, and smile condescendingly at the heavier folk who had the misfortune of thinking they should get some regular exercise.

Women golfers never wear thongs, skintight leotards, and leopard halters. These clothes are not designed for real sports. They were made by men so that a woman who weighs more than 103 pounds or who has less than a 36E bosom will feel lucky that she has a husband or boyfriend, even if he is a real creep. Golfers are feminists; they don't wear those kinds of clothes.

Aerobic dancers are also greedy. Whoever saw a woman golfer point to some imaginary line on the red tee box and say, "Do you mind moving over? This is my spot. I was here first. I stopped by when I first got here, before I went to the bathroom, changed into these clothes, and stopped to talk to Jane." She points to a water bottle against the wall twenty feet from where you are standing. "See? My water bottle is even here."

Except for an abnormal preoccupation with the aerobic laws on space ownership, aerobic exercisers never talk. Before class, they are too busy stretching their size-4 tummies or primping their hair into cute little ponytails. During class, they may let out an occasional shout after their instructor tells them to, but it is never a real conversation. Then, after class, they are too busy to talk because they want to rush off to get ready for their dates or to eat their 350-calorie dinners.

Women golfers, on the other hand, are always ready to share

some talk and a beer on the nineteenth hole. Perhaps most positive, they never, never shout on command. In fact, they command so much presence not even a pro would ask them to.

One of the reasons they command this respect is that women golfers are very intelligent. They are much, much smarter than aerobic dancers. Admittedly, a woman golfer may need to get tips from a pro once in a while. No pro has ever been required to keep reminding a golfer to keep breathing, however. Yet that is a standard command by the aerobics instructor. "Don't forget to breathe!!" Aerobic dancers apparently have such little concentration they can't do two things at the same time.

Skiers

Skiers are no challenge in the golfer girlfriend contest. Skiers slide down mountains in cold weather on pieces of wood not very much wider than the shaft of a golf club. The cold adversely affects their outlook, making them the least optimistic of all athletes. In fact, sad to say, they spend the major part of their first years of training learning how to fall. What golfer would waste her time learning how to recover from an overwound swing?

"Let's see, I want to avoid falling face-first at all costs—I could break my neck. Should I fall gently to the side into the red tees or backward onto my clubs?"

Skiers are very unkind. They make fun of each other, using

derogatory terms such as the "dope slope." Golfers, on the other hand, are too noble to be mean. They call dope courses "executive courses" and dunce tees "gold tees."

Skiers have no appreciation for etiquette. They have little concern about remaining quiet while the skiers next to them get ready to hit the slopes. Skiers don't care if they disturb the people around them. They also don't care about nature. It does not matter how much the earth is hurting; no skier ever worries about any ninety-degree rule. All they care about is getting down the mountain.

It is true that they zigzag down the mountain. This is not because they are trying to preserve the environment, however. It is because they deliberately engage in slow play! Men skiers do not discriminate against women skiers the way men golfers do against women golfers, though. Did you ever hear of a men-only Saturday slope?

The reason for this is that women skiers cater to men. Every woman skier starves herself so that she will be thin. Women skiers say they have to stay in shape to engage in the sport. Women golfers know the truth about women skiers, though. They diet constantly, because they want to look better than everyone else. Why else would they wear those skintight flamboyant pants with matching jackets for the opportunity to break their legs? Also, why else do they spend so much time primping to sit in front of a fireplace at a jazzed-up skier's nineteenth hole?

Let's face it, women skiers are loose women. Also, just about every one is an alcoholic. The only reason skiers ski is they want to have an excuse to have a scotch and soda in the lodge afterward. Their idea of a marshal is a St. Bernard with a "lifesaving" barrel of brandy. Golfers, on the other hand, usually drink beer, and they only drink *that* when they are playing very well or very poorly or if it's just an average day. Women golfers make the best friends.

Sailors

Sailors do not make good friends. Sailors are very competitive by nature, and they engage in highly questionable behavior. For instance, unlike golfers who just like to play fast, sailors like to race. When they are in a race, they deliberately try to position their vessel so as to block the wind from the sails of their opponents.

Contrast that with the golfer. Who ever saw a woman golfer recklessly cut her golf cart in front of her opponents? Moreover, even when playing in a $200,000 tournament, she absolutely will make sure that not even her shadow falls on the path of your putt!

Sailors are also very loud people. They like to shout orders to each other as they try to outdo each other in sailor talk. Who ever heard a golfer yell at the top of her lungs to her partner, "Dogleg left ahead! Prepare to hook! Hook-ho!" Sailors think nothing, however, of prefacing every intended motion of their vessel with preparatory commands obvious to everyone who hasn't fallen overboard.

Golfers respect the concentration necessary for successful performance by other athletes and remain silent when the people accompanying them prepare to play.

To be fair, both sailors and golfers have similar concerns about the environment and seek to understand nature for their own good. Wind must be calculated and lightning avoided by each at all costs. Of course, this is a lot easier for sailors than it is for golfers. In bad weather, sailors can always refrain from going out, or, if they are out, head for port or go below. Golfers have a tee time to meet and a strict four-hour-and-twenty-minute objective.

If you like loud, obnoxious, controlling friends, you might like sailors. Otherwise you will find that women golfers make the best friends.

Ladies' Leagues

There are two kinds of ladies' leagues. There are business golf leagues, and there are country-club golf leagues.

Business golf leagues have tournaments on weekends and play nights after work. Country-club golf leagues have tournaments and play days on Tuesday and Wednesday mornings.

Women join business golf leagues to meet other women golfers and so that they will get good enough to play with the men golfers with whom they work. Women golfers remain in these leagues because they like playing golf with other women, they

enjoy networking with women who may be good business contacts, and men golfers would rather play with men than women
anyway.

Women join country-club golf leagues to meet other women
golfers and so that they will get good enough to play with their
husbands. Women golfers remain in these leagues because they
like playing golf with other women, they enjoy networking with
women whose husbands may be good business contacts for their
husbands, and their husbands would rather play with men than
women anyway.

Women who join business golf leagues and women who join
country-club leagues do not play golf together. With so little in
common, what would they find to talk about?

The Social Science of Golf

To win at the social game of golf you need more than a good swing,
a decent putt, and a flat ball marker. Golf is like business.
Competence may be important, but to really succeed you must be
politically adept.

Few golfers have the luxury or loneliness of playing the game
alone. It is essential for a golfer to understand that there is more to
the game than playing yourself. You must play yourself when you
are playing with, or at least among, others.

Some golfers may find the easiest way to do this is to just

show up on a course and wait for the starter to pair you up with someone. Most women golfers do not prefer this social option, however. "It's more fun to play golf with people you know," say most women golfers.

Let's face it. Starters don't care if the person they pair you up with has a habit of looking at every shot from every angle and then blaming you for playing slow. Starters also don't care if the only thing you have in common with the person you're about to spend four and a half hours with is that you each wish you were spending that time with someone else.

Now, there is the occasional extrovert among us. You may find a woman who likes the excitement of hitting an embarrassing forty-yard slice in front of three golfers who wish she weren't there. Most of us women golfers, however, prefer to put together our own groups. Our attitude is, "I only want people I know and like to say how lousy I golf."

Given the large number of women golfers today, it should be easy for us to put together foursomes, yet it is not. Setting up a successful golf game is similar to putting together a good dinner party. Everyone may eat, but not everyone eats together well.

In golf, as in a dinner party, your goal is to get together a group of people who challenge each other as well as themselves and who claim to have a great time as they are doing so. It is fun to invite people in different professions or who have different backgrounds; it is disastrous to invite people who do not practice the same etiquette. You will be just as comfortable inviting a golfer to your course who doesn't take care of her pitch marks on the green as you are inviting a diner to your clubhouse who burps long and loudly after each meal.

In golf, as in a dinner party, it is important to invite the right number of guests. You can't invite more guests than your available tea or tee times permit. An even number of participants is also preferred. No one likes to be paired up with his or her shadow. Yes, the rules for setting up a game are simple. The divots, however, are in the details. Just think of what you must do to go golfing this Saturday.

You must first call for a tee time at the club where you want to play. This is a simple matter, or at least it is if you get up at 5:00 A.M. the first day on which you are eligible to register at that club for an advance tee time.

This does not mean you will get the time you want. It will, however, give you some waggle room. For instance, if the pro tells you he cannot give you a foursome at ten o'clock, you might check to see if he can give you a twosome then. If the club has two or three courses, maybe one of the alternate courses is available at the time you hoped to play. Few of us women leave the whole matter to pro-shop voodoo. We throw at least a little of our own magic dust into the process—maybe an extra five-dollar bill, too. Ultimately, being the smart golfer you are, you have a tee time.

Having successfully negotiated a tee time, you are ready to stop dealing with strangers and to start haggling with friends. Golf is very much a skills game. One of the most difficult skills in golf gamesmanship is learning how to invite your friends to play golf on a conditional basis and getting them to accept on an unconditional basis. That is because they always try to achieve the opposite.

Think of what happens when you try to fill your foursome. You call your best friend. "Sue, I just a got a tee time for Saturday at ten o'clock. Do you want to play?"

"Yes, I would love to play, but can I let you know Friday night? My in-laws are thinking of spending this weekend with us. I don't think they will; they always make plans and never keep them. But I had better not commit to you yet," Sue answers.

"Okay. I'll put together the rest of our foursome. Just promise you'll let me know as soon as possible," you respond.

Now whom should you invite? Hey, how about Mary and Lynne? You call them both. Their respective answering machines respond. You leave them each the same message. "Do you want to play golf on Saturday? I have a tee time at ten o'clock at the Ranch. Call me and let me know."

You wait. Tuesday and Wednesday go by. No return calls from Mary or Lynne. It is now Thursday morning. You call them again.

Mary is home. "Oh, I was just planning to call you. I have the flu. I hope to get over it. I'll let you know tomorrow, okay?"

Lynne does not answer her home phone. You call her office and find out that she is out of town until Saturday morning.

Thursday afternoon comes. Mary calls. "Hi, I'm still sick. I hope you can find someone else." You hope you can, too.

Should you ask that woman you met at the club? The one you thought you might like? What about Joanne? She's so much fun. Would it be rude to invite Joanne and not Jane? They always play together. Of course, if one of your other potential players decides not to play, Jane could play, too. Maybe you should call Lisa. You haven't played with her for a while.

You call Joanne, Jane, and Lisa. None of them is home. You leave the same message on each of their answering machines. "I have a tee time at ten o'clock on Saturday. Give me a call and let me know if you want to play."

None of them calls you back Thursday night. On Friday morning, two of the three call to accept. Sue, your best friend, calls Friday night and says she'll be there, too.

Wow! you think. What a great foursome! We are going to have such a good time!

Saturday morning Lynne calls and says she is back from her trip and can play. Oh, shoot. "I didn't hear from you, Lynne, so I invited someone else. Of course, if you really want to play, I'll see if I can get another group together, or you can go in my place."

She doesn't take you up on your offer. No wonder you like her so much!

Just when you are heading to the course, Sue calls and cancels. You call Lynne back. "You won't believe it, but Sue just canceled out. Her undependable in-laws came into town. Hope you can still make it!" She can.

When you get to the course, the other members of your foursome are already there. What fun! Everyone is impressed that you put together such a great group. The adeptness of your planning is evident.

Why not? You know the ropes. Had only three golfers shown up you would have insisted on riding alone. That would, after all, have given you some time alone to figure out who else you should have called. Had there been just two of you, you would have told your partner how delighted you were to share the afternoon with her (and the two fat, balding men you were paired up with who now are giving you dirty looks).

If you had a fivesome...if you had a fivesome you would have incurred the wrath of every golfer on the course, including the former friends in your fivesome. Putting together a fivesome is like arranging a blind date between two people who just got divorced—from each other. It's not done.

"What do you like best about golf?" Lynne asks you.

"It's just so-o-o relaxing," you reply. "You don't have to worry about anything in the world except that little white ball."

Taking Golf Trips

Pros claim it is good for your game to play the same course all the time. They say it allows you to play with concentration and without the distraction of figuring out distances over obstacles and to greens. We women golfers know better, however.

Every woman golfer enjoys the challenge of a different course. How exciting to see for the first time a line of church-pew sand traps and then avoid every one of them! How soothing to have a distance miscalculation, rather than a lousy swing, be the reason a ball impolitely plops right into water.

The greens are always grassier and the clubhouse always classier the farther the golf course is from home. Committed women golfers thus are driven (and putted) to go on at least one golfing trip each year. By this, I mean a legitimate golfing trip. A legitimate golfing trip is a trip taken explicitly for golf—more explicitly, for *her* golf. A legitimate golfing trip is taken solely with other women. No men or children are allowed.

This does not mean a woman will not enjoy a trip to the Caribbean to hit the sticks with her date or mate. That trip, however, cannot serve as a substitute for the woman's annual golfing trip.

A woman's first annual golfing trip starts like any other tradition. It is not yet one. Thus, that first golfing trip carries a much different set of expectations than will subsequent journeys. On her first trip, a woman may attend an organized weekend excursion with her league or a highly touted all women's golf-weekend school. The key is that someone else—someone official—organizes it. The woman merely attends.

"Now, this is heaven!"

A woman's first golfing trip is usually at most a five-hour drive from home. Usually her best golfing buddies are also going. When invited, she may feel a little bit guilty about leaving her husband, kids, or dogs to fend for themselves. Yet the sheer excitement of a weekend doing nothing but golfing weaves its spell. Voila! (or perhaps more aptly put, Fore!). She is going golfing.

Usually, this will require some explanation. "No," she again tells the surprised members of her family, "this is not a business trip." Indeed, the sole purpose for her sojourn is to spend even more of her time chasing after those little white balls.

"It's only one night," she reminds herself —and him—as she packs an extra box of golf balls, her new golfing attire, and (what the heck?) a giant thermos of margaritas in her overnight bag. She is right. It is only one night. On that first trip, that is. The second trip will be longer—maybe an extra night or two. Maybe this time she will take some puddlejumper flight to reach her destination. She'll just split the cost of the car rental with her golfing partner. "After all," she reasons, "I can probably get in at least one more round of golf if we fly instead of drive. I might as well make full use of my time while I am away."

In year three, she does not need to explain her decision to go on a trip to her date or mate. It is, after all, a tradition. It is something she does at least once every year. It is like Christmas or Thanksgiving. You can count on it. She does.

Traditions are ironic. Traditions are traditions only because of their sameness, yet we choose to celebrate traditions by their uniqueness. In carrying on a bona fide tradition, it is essential that the quality of the celebration in some way be just a little bit better than it was last time.

Therefore, a woman measures her third-year golfing trip in weeks rather than days. If she played golf at some inexpensive course in New Hampshire last year, this year it will be a week at the Broadmoor in Colorado. Or say she spends a week visiting the top-notch courses in the Carolinas this year. Next year, then, she just may take one of those standard three-week, $10,000 Australian golfing excursions. She still will have things to look forward to. Maybe down the road she could spend a month or two in Scotland exploring the origins of golf.

Men golfers never understand the average woman golfer's need to roam. They ask each other, "Why would someone with a 20 or 25 handicap seek out the most difficult courses she can find and pay the exorbitant tourist rates those courses demand?" The answer, however, is obvious. How else can she buy those cute little tags of the signature holes of each course, custom-engraved with the names of the friends and family members she left behind?

This does not imply that we women are not serious about golf on our trips. Indeed, the game is paramount. You don't have to take my word on this, either. Ask the golf-course manager who pays the printing charges for golf scorecards. He knows how committed we women are to discovering the course, documenting our successes and failures on it, and sharing our golf experience with everyone in our league.

In fact, the very first thing we do when we visit a resort course is to pick up that course's scorecards. We need a lot of them, too. Let's see. We need one to study in the lunchroom before the game; one for turning in our handicap; one on which to record everyone's score; and one on which to keep only our score and its components (the number of fairways hit, number of penalty shots, number of putts, number of pitches, number of whiffs, number of sand traps hit, and the number of things to keep track of). Oh, yeah, and four or five to bring home to our friends.

At the pro shop, we seem obsessed about our score, because of the large number of scorecards we take. Scoring low is not even an important element of this golf outing, though (unless, of course, we do). We women may track our scores on the four or five scorecards we have, but our real goal on golf trips is to make those really good shots. You know, the kind we can talk about in the nineteenth hole afterward.

The golfer on vacation does not go for percentage shots, unless, of course, that percentage happens to be 20 percent or less. What glory is there in playing the most difficult course we could both get on and afford to play, only to shoot five to ten strokes above our handicaps?

It is much more fulfilling to disregard the score—unless it is very, very good—and focus on the development of those career shots. How exciting to hit a ball 160 yards over water from a very poor lie situated right behind a waterfall! So what if it was your fifth shot that made it. Who is going to know that part of the story anyway?

The need for success stories becomes increasingly obvious to each vacationing woman golfer as the eighteenth hole draws nearer. After all, golfing expeditions are not a single-sport adventure. Drinking is also ambitiously pursued. Of course, the best way to enjoy that activity is to supplement it with spicy foods and even spicier stories.

Pretend you are on a trip. You walk into the nineteenth hole. You and the other members of your foursome approach the women who teed off right before you.

"You should have seen my drive on the third hole!" one of the ladies says to you. "It was the funniest shot I ever saw," recalls her cart mate. "Her ball hit a tree on the left-hand side of the course, landed on a rock on the right, bounced off and hit the water, bounced out—did you hear me?—actually bounced out of the water, and then landed ninety yards from the green, right in the middle of the fairway!"

How are you going to respond? "That's cool. Oh, I shot only twelve strokes over my handicap." Exciting, huh?

In the nineteenth hole of a resort club, scores are merely numbers. The winning is in the stories. Women on trips thus just "go for it." That applies to off the course, as well as on. Women golfers on vacation sparkle with the spirit of self-actualization. We may visit a spa, take a mudbath, get a massage, take a spur-of-the-moment $150 session with a local pro, or just plain shop.

Women on golfing trips do not act like men on golfing trips. Men golfers on vacation play thirty-six holes a day and then sit around in their condos at night, drinking beer, playing cards, and telling dirty stories and dirtier jokes. We women are different. We don't drink beer. We prefer wine or margaritas.

Of course, the women's golfing trip does not come cheap. We have to find someplace to pinch some pennies. Most of us save money by reducing the number of long-distance phone calls we make. Sure, our mates miss hearing from us, but they understand. Each woman's schedule is so busy. If she is going to call and chat very long, she will have to miss one of her activities. The most logical one, of course, would be the dirty-joke swap. Her mate surely does not want her to miss that. Where else is he going to get some good material for his next golf trip?

Gentlewomanly Competition

All women are not equally noncompetitive. Some women golfers thrive on the competitive nature of golf. A competitive woman may play golf year round, yet she plays golf for only one season—the tournament season.

A competitive woman golfer is the kind of woman who

becomes upset if her opponents use a foot wedge to kick their balls from behind a tree or if they discount their whiffs as practice swings. A competitive woman golfer expects her opponents to play by the rules and herself to play around them. A competitive woman golfer, in other words, is a real golfer.

Competitive women are women who golf to win. Women who golf to win like to golf with other women who golf to win. Competitive women thus participate in all kinds of competitions.

Four-Person Scrambles

Competitive women are easy to spot in scrambles. They are not the ones who identify "cart driving" as their strength and "ball driving" as their weakness, when asked by their team captain what they expect to contribute to their team's scramble. Competitive women golfers are the ones who are more interested in knowing everyone's handicap than where they can buy more beer.

A noncompetitive woman competing in a scramble is happy when her team chooses her ball to play. She does not care if it was because her ball was the only ball that landed in bounds. The important point to her is that the team is using her ball. It is just darn lucky she is playing today.

A competitive woman golfer, however, sees the broader picture. This is not some cordial foursome. This is not a private outing. This is a competition. Their (her!) scores will be posted, for heaven's sake!

Thus, the competitive woman who hits a lousy drive—which her team uses because everyone else's sliced into the woods—is not happy. It is bad enough that she did not get under the ball. To be stuck with three other people who can't hit the ball worth a darn is, however, almost unbearable.

The competitive woman golfer does not join in the lively discussion her teammates are having about the sale at their favorite golf store. Instead, she wants to motivate her team to play well.

"We don't deserve any more golf equipment if we keep playing like this," she admonishes them. "You would think at least one of us would have had a longer drive. Oh well," she comments as they proceed the forty yards from the red tees to take their next shot. "It doesn't take us out of the running. We could still win. All we have to do is concentrate."

"Great!" answers her noncompetitive cart mate.

"Hey," says another teammate, pointing to a large bird over-head. "That looks like a vulture."

"Yeah, well it is going to eat our lunch if we don't concentrate on our game," says the woman who likes to win.

"Oh, who cares? The prize is only some socks or balls anyway," responds the other.

The competitive woman, however, knows differently. The prize for winning is winning.

"I'm tired of these Florida scrambles!"

Two-Person Scrambles

A competitive woman prefers two-person scrambles to four people scrambling. With a two-person scramble, there is only one person, other than herself, who can screw things up. She also usually has more control over who her partner will be. She wants someone competitive—someone like herself.

Foursomes with two-person scrambles are always very sociable on the first tee box. That may be, after all, the last time each will talk to the competition. Oh, sure, women playing in a two-person team may occasionally interact with their opponents. They may cajole the other team a little bit or make some joking remarks about how happy they are to have their cart mate as a "partner." Most of their talk is reserved for their teammate, though—especially if they are losing.

Competitive women love to have a partner when they are losing. This is not just because they want someone to blame, either. It is so reassuring to have someone to confide in that the only reason the other team is scoring better is because they are cheating.

The competitive woman who keeps losing will thus start counting the other team's strokes as well as her own. Even if it all checks out, as is usually the case, she will at least have won at something today. She got that other team to stop cheating before she caught them, didn't she?

Individual Medal Play

Whoever thinks golf is fun has never played in a woman's club championship. Club championships make every woman competitive. Competitive women in medal-play golf behave the way men do all the time. They act cordial, play mean, and feel vicious.

Oh, good, the competitive woman thinks when her opponent hits a stump that causes her ball to ricochet into the lake. She does not hide her feelings from her opponent. She could cheer up her opponent with a casual comment, such as "Hey, bad luck!" She does not, though. No, she will not say anything at all. If someone asks her about it later, she'll just say she didn't notice. In fact, she will say, "I thought my opponent was pretty darn lucky all day."

Competitive women seldom talk to each other as they compete. They also never talk to each other's balls. No way is the competitive woman going to yell at her opponent's ball, "In the water, in the water!" when it looks as if that is precisely where it may go. She just has too much class to scream out her strongest desires.

The only discussion between opponents in serious medal play involves potential breaches of etiquette. The competitive woman, for instance, may give her opponent a break. "From the angle in which I am standing, it looks as if your big toe may be a quarter-of-an-inch or more in front of that red tee box indicator which has fallen over. It really doesn't matter to me, of course. I would,

however, hate to see you get called on it." She thus calls her on it but pretends to be a good guy while she is doing it.

The most social aspect of medal play is ordering water from the beverage-cart woman. "I'll take that loaded. With lemon, that is," you joke. Yup, competitive play really rolls in comedy.

In a club championship you have no friends. There is you, your ball, your clubs, and—thank the golf gods—your handicap. That's why I think competitive women like themselves more than most women do. You really have to enjoy your own company to maintain such solitude through eighteen holes. It makes me lonely. I even start missing all that great advice I get when I play with men.

Seventh Hole:

Women Enjoy the Game

A Hole in One Is Better Than Your Ordinary Orgasm

Women play golf because they enjoy it. It is, after all, much more natural than sex.

If you are like most people, you may find this hard to believe. So, go ahead. Stop by the magazine rack or self-help section of any bookstore. You'll find loads of literature for sale on how a woman can achieve an orgasm through the normal mating process. However, did you ever see a book on how she can feel good after a hole in one?

That's not proof enough? Well then, visit your favorite golfing fanatic at work. Spend the day with her. Listen to how many times golf comes up in her conversations. If you pretend you're not looking, sometime that day you'll see her take a practice swing or two, or at least a couple of waggles, with an imaginary club. Her grip will be in place; her approach will be correct; the only golfing items missing are her clubs, balls, and a golf course.

Now ask yourself, How many times that day did she practice the missionary position in her office? How many times did she begin a conversation with even her closest colleagues, "Hey, have you had any good sex lately?"

Those experts who say people daydream about sex 20 percent of the time when they are not having it can't help you. They have no credibility. How do they know what someone is thinking? Furthermore, even if what they say is true, the fact that a person may daydream about sex proves nothing. Golfers have their dreams, too. In fact, every golfer, regardless of gender, religion, race, national origin, or handicap, also has a dream...a dream of a hole in one.

Usually a golfer has this dream when standing on the tee box of a par-3 that has a 120-yard very wet chasm in front of the green, four sand traps around the green, and an undulating green that promises a roller-coaster ride to every ball that lands on it. "If only that ball would go in that hole," she thinks.

Her cart mate feels the same way. "Hit that baby right in the hole!" he yells (especially if he just hit his into the drink). And why not? Golf is like that. If you can't get your own ball up, voyeurism is your next best option.

Having a hole in one is better than your ordinary orgasm. If you have a hole in one, you can have your achievement published in at least three golf newspapers or journals. You can buy a plaque, suitable for hanging in your office, that has a picture of you at the hole, the actual ball you struck, and a description of the hole that graced your game. You can join a club that only people who have had holes in one can join. Also, you can mention it casually every time you play golf to everyone who has heard the story less than twenty times. If you have a hole in one, everyone, without exception, will know you hit one wonderful shot.

If you have an orgasm, you can't publish it in the paper. That would be considered provocative. You can't advertise your success on a plaque and hang it up in your office. That would be considered grounds for termination. You could join a club, but it would not be exclusive. Even virgins can join a hot-tub club, for instance. Most important, you can't even tell anyone, except the person you were with, that you had an orgasm. The last straw is that conventional heterosexual etiquette dictates that, rather than telling the man you were with how great you were, you should instead give him all the credit and tell him how great he was.

Having an orgasm thus just does not lead to the public recognition an ace does. Not that hole-in-one achievers are publicity hounds. Sure, it is nice to have the world acknowledge your achievements; but that is not the force that drives golfers (and their balls) to holes in one.

After all, everyone knows that not all acers are great golfers. Beginners have holes in one. Double-bogey golfers have holes in one. Pros have holes in one. Thus, while your hole in one may be attributed to your outstanding skills, a few doubters may say it was caused by luck instead.

Even lovers will tell you, however, that being lucky is not a bad thing. In fact, being lucky is actually something to brag about. Luck is the kiss of fortune. It is the smile of fate. It is the water your ball skips on and the branch your ball misses. Some people may think of luck as unfair at best, and at its worst, as something you can't claim as your own.

"She was just lucky," someone might say. Golfers know, however, there is no "just" in luck. Luck is an attraction that brings good things your way. Luck is as important to a golfer as charm is to a lover.

"Oh my, the ball went right into the hole!" exclaims the excited golfer as she jumps up and down and watches her first hole in one. "Unbelievable!" She marks "1" on her scorecard. She will keep this scorecard the rest of her life. She will also play golf the rest of her life. Or at least until she is ninety. Maybe I'll get another one! she thinks.

A hole in one is both satisfying and seducing. It can be a little more dangerous than your ordinary orgasm. After all, you may have heard people talk about free love, but how often have you seen the expression "free golf"?

That's not all bad either, though. Most courses are as crowded as an orgy anyway.

Prayers to the Golf Goddess

I was in the middle of a tournament. I lined up to hit my ball over to the other side of a 130-yard creek. Shoot! I hit it fat! "Oh, let my ball be up!" I say as my cart-mate competitor drives me over to the other side to look for my ball. We just couldn't tell if it made it over or not. Wait a minute! There it is! My ball is resting in a good lie five yards from the green. My competitor looks up toward the heavens, shakes her fist, and yells to that most accommodating golf god, "Do that again and she'll be disqualified for divine intervention!"

There is no such thing as luck on the golf course. The golf gods either like you or they don't. You may think that you can buy favor by wearing soft spikes, refilling your divots, and gracing the greens. Yet the golf gods still may end the flight of your finely shot ball with a branch five feet longer and ten feet lower than it was when you hit that same tree branch last week.

The golf gods favor beginners and juniors, both of whom are much more apt to become entranced with the magic of the game than the addition of their score. They also fulfill the expectation of every golfer who hits a couple of poor shots and then thinks her game is shot.

If, however, you can mentally release the shot where your ball unexpectedly hit a three-inch invisible tree branch, then bounced across the cart path to dive into the water, the golf gods still may not favor you. Yet, so what? With that kind of mental discipline, why would you need them anyway?

All women know there is no golf god, only a goddess. Only a woman could think up a game that people play to get exercise, requires a cart to ride in, features a pub in which to eat and drink afterward, and has an incentive system which rewards those who complete the session with the least possible effort.

There is no such thing as an atheist in a sand trap. My pro had a favorite prayer for use on the golf course. It was an original prayer. She composed it herself when she took up the game and has been relying on it ever since. She said it has about a 50-percent effective rate for her putts and about a 25-percent effective rate on her drives. It works better when she is winning than when she is losing. She shared it with me so I'll share it with you. This is it: "Just this once, let me hit this ball just right. And if I do, I promise, I promise that I will never, ever ask You for anything else again."

My favorite golf partners are ministers, priests, and rabbis. I figure that way I'll have a partner in the inner circle in the event we start praying for a small miracle.

Charity Golf Makes Golfers Charitable

Everyone who plays in a charity golf tournament is rich, wanna-be rich, or employed by a corporation that is rich. Everyone who plays in a charity tournament thus has some green, but not every one of them knows how to make the green.

Charity golfers tend to be lousy golfers but gracious losers. Charity golf tournaments are the only tournaments in which a golfer with a disgustingly poor swing can compete without someone paired up with him whining, "He shouldn't have come if he can't play any better than that."

Most charity tournaments, of course, are in the four-person scramble format. This is the format that is most conducive to getting three terrible players and one good one through eighteen holes of shanks, slices, wormburners, and cloudteasers in eight hours or less.

Usually, the A player decides which ball to play while the B, C, and D players wish that at least once it could be one of theirs. Scores over par are routinely posted in four-person charity scrambles, and those scores may not reflect anything about how poor the real score is. Most charity golfers are too honest to deliberately cheat. Yet they are also too inexperienced to keep score accurately . If their A player says they will take a gimme, Mr. B will record a score indicating that their last putt went into the hole. If their A player tells them they can place their ball a club's length away from the best shot in their foursome, Mr. B, C, and D will use the clubhouse as their measuring stick. The A player will not even bother correcting this 300-yard mistake. He figures, What chance do we have of winning anyway?

Women golfers do not play as much charity golf as men. It is not because women are not eligible. There are, after all, a lot of lousy women golfers too. The reason very few women play charity golf is that businesses usually pay the entry fees for charity golfers, and businesses usually choose men rather than women golfers to lose the tournament for them.

Playing in a charity tournament costs $150 to $15,000. The entry fee includes a round of golf at a course whose greens fees on noncharity days range from $20 to $200; a dinner at least as elegant as a Big Mac with fries; and usually a silent auction during dinner. Charity tournaments prefer silent auctions. I guess they realize that by the time the golfers come in to eat their dinner, their throats are too sore from yelling "Fore!" to permit them to bid out loud.

Charity tournaments are expensive, as they should be. Charity tournaments are not about golf; they are about raising money for some good cause. In fact, many of the golfers who play in them even know what the cause is. By this, I mean the cause other than the company's getting a tax deduction and their getting out of work all day at company expense.

Playing golf at a charity tournament should never be considered a decadent act. You are, after all, doing something good for somebody. It's a little like giving blood, but involves fewer complications. At a golf tournament, you don't have to answer a bunch of questions to which you don't know the answer. You don't, for instance, need to know if you ever dated a man who dated a woman who dated a man who fell in love with a prostitute. In fact, most charity golfers face only one unanswerable question. It is the dreaded, "What is your handicap?"

It's a shame more women do not play in charitable events. It makes it very difficult for the few who do. At the start of the competition, men look at women playing in a charity tournament as if, were it not for this woman assigned to their team, they might actually have a chance of winning. Only later will they learn that they should attribute their loss to the fact that their team is composed of men who said they had 25 handicaps only because the guy in front of them did.

Regardless of the quality of the play, however, the quality of the players can be exceedingly high at charity tournaments. In fact, these golfers are downright charitable. Charity golfers will usually rejoice when a woman is assigned to their foursome, once they realize that she can play from the tees that at least two of the other players in their foursome (always the other two) should be using.

Charity golfers play slowly. Their games usually last five and one-half hours to seven hours. This is one of the reasons the rules of golf are relaxed for them. Imagine how long they would take if every foursome actually had to go back to its former position every time all four players hit out-of-bounds.

Of course, some of the more prestigious tournaments actually have players who follow the rules and can hit the ball. These may raise more money than the others, but they seldom raise as much fun. After all, the charm in charity tournaments is the players who have hearts of gold and nerves of steel but who have never heard of clubs of titanium or, at least, have never played with them.

Charity golf gives golfers a chance to develop a feel for more than their putters. It also gives them a chance to get in touch with their souls.

Home on the Range

Give me a course
where my balls don't roam
while my opponents' balls go astray...

Why do so few women feel at home on the driving range? Why does the range remain largely a man's province, even today, when there are more than five million women golfers?

One reason is that men are more willing to work at making power shots off the tee. Another reason is that once men learn how to make power shots, they can't control them. All of their drives start going out-of-bounds. Then they need to go practice them. The biggest reason, though, is that women tend to like to golf in groups, and the range is for lone wolves.

Companionship is an important part of the golfing experience for a woman. Women go to the course not only to golf, but also to discuss their lives. They talk about their careers, their families, their hopes, their fears, and (sometimes) their game. The cadence of the game is such that other players' tee shots are times of reflection. They are times built into the game to meditate on what has been discussed, so that the conversation or the shared silence can continue when the shots are made.

This natural rhythm is destroyed on the driving range. The range is just a series of tee shots. On a golf course, private discussions and reflections take place, interrupted by brief episodes of strokes; on the range, round after round of shots follow round after round of shots.

Women enjoy the space between the shots. Just as music has been said to be composed of the moments between the notes, golf, to many women, is the walk between the swings.

We can get as poetic as we want, but we still must recognize one fact. Men practice more than women do, and they probably get more effective practice because of their consistent use of the driving range. This practice pays off for them on the golf course. After constantly hitting ball after ball on the range, men think nothing of taking mulligan after mulligan. A woman would feel as if she were cheating. A man, on the other hand, lives the adage "Practice makes perfect." Men thus become dedicated to their tee shots; women merely are dedicated to the game.

For Every Season There Is a Time...for Women to Golf

Spring

You begin thinking of slipping out of the office a couple of hours early...

You start planning the golf season ahead...

The call of the ball...

Lots of telephone calls, too!

Spring! It's that time of year when we women golfers dust off our golfing directories and start putting some foursomes together.

"Four for Fore!"

"Gotta get a tee time before 1:30 to get in eighteen holes," we remind each other as we schedule Sunday's game.

Spring! It's that time of year when we explain to our date or mate why we will be unavailable every Saturday and Sunday afternoon until winter.

Spring. It's a magical time of year when every bad shot, be it a slice, whiff, wormburner, pull, shank, hook, or rainmaker, is caused by the very same reason—winter.

Of course, women golfers do more than play on the golf course this time of year. There is a lot of spring cleaning for them to do. Let's see, maybe you should get rid of that old set of clubs and buy a new set. Or how about trading in that putter or driver for one that works?

The need for new clubs is most obvious to those golfers who spent their winters at inside driving ranges. Those balls just are not going the 220 yards they imagined they would. This is the case even though they had consistently hit them that far in their mind as they swiped their balls ten feet into a net at their favorite inside range. Must have worn out their clubs with all that good practice!

Spring is the beginning of the golf season. It is a time women set goals for their play, too. I like to set stretch goals. For instance, last spring I decided I wanted to play as well as most men think I think they play.

Summer

Hot steamy summer days...

Days on which women golfers, particularly those in warm climates, joke about the ninety-degree rule...

"Don't play golf if it is over ninety degrees."

"Use a cart if it is over ninety degrees."

Every woman golfer knows, though, that even a dog day in summer is a good day to golf. After all, the heat scares off many of those slow men golfers. It also gives the one or two slow women golfers out there a reason to play slowly.

Getting an early tee time—when it is cooler outside—becomes the most popular off-the-golf-course sport. Acquaintances who consistently get 8:30 A.M. tee times become best friends. Nongolfing friends become "old" friends—that is, the kind of friends who are good to get together with on rainy days, on dark nights, and in the winter.

Of course, it is not the woman golfer's fault. Women golfers go out of their way to salvage their winter friendships with their nongolfing buddies, be it summer or any other time of year. They encourage their clubless pals to take up the game. They even utilize their creative gift-giving skills by buying beginning golf books as birthday presents for these people who never have swung a club nor had any interest in doing so.

Let's face it, though. Summer is no time to take up the game. Women golfers may yearn for summer all year long, because they believe it is the best time to golf. The truth is, however, it is tougher to play golf in the summer than at any other time of year. By summer, all of the trees and bushes are filled out and the grass is thick—so thick you do not get the slick run of the ball that you get on dry winter grass or ice.

As a result, women golfers in the know avoid playing with men in the summer. They recognize that men are the ones who make those long drives into the woods and then cannot get their balls out because of the leaf-filled branches. A man then will drop a ball 300 yards from the white tees, right in the middle of the fairway, because he is pretty sure he saw his ball hit one of those trees, boomerang across forty yards, and land directly in front of the hole. "Well, it's not my fault the #$%@! grass is so thick that the ball got lost," he says.

Summer golf has its challenges, but the truth is that it also has its conveniences. By the summer, every woman golfer is ready to play at the simple drop of a sun visor. She keeps her golfing clothes and golf bag at the club or in her car, just in case there is time for an unexpected nine holes. Let me tell you, that bag is ready to go, with balls, tees, golf shoes, golf clothes—absolutely everything necessary—present and accounted for. That is, except for the woman golfer herself. She is absent, curiously absent, from work and home.

Fall

Most people associate fall with football. Women golfers do, too. Women golfers love men who love football.

Football games pretty much guarantee the availability of tee times, as well as the elimination of at least half of the male population from the golf course. Women may be physically present on the golf course during a big football game, but do not let that fool you. No one, no one, roots more avidly for their home football team than women. After all, if the local gridiron contenders have a winning streak, that will really empty the golf course on football days.

Those empty golf courses help the woman golfer's game, too. Let's face it, ladies, men are people you might prefer not to play with, but whom you surely don't want to play behind. Men think that because they swing faster than women, they play faster. Unfortunately, it does not matter if they swing 100 miles an hour. Those six practice shots before they do so get on the clock, too.

So fall is the time of the year when a woman's game is at its best. Maybe this fall she will break one hundred, ninety, or even eighty! If nothing else, by fall she has broken her piggy bank trying to get there. Furthermore, she has every reason to believe she will play even better next year, given the assurances regarding her vast improvement she has received from her highly paid pro and her three best golfing buddies.

Of course, the absence of men on the course is not the only reason a woman plays better golf in the fall. Probably the major reason is that by fall women play more like men. The reason for this, of course, is that by fall they have played with men perhaps more times than they wanted.

In any event, by fall the woman golfer who has played often with men has started to pick up some of the real tricks of the game. For instance, she has learned how to overcome obstacles. Her ball flies into a sand trap. No problem. If there is a trickle of water, it becomes an unnatural hazard, and she gets to drop it outside the trap. Or let's say she has trouble finding her ball in the fall fairway landscape, with all those leaves on the ground. Again, no problem.

By fall she has learned to follow the flight of her ball very carefully, just as the men she has played with do, and she now can closely estimate, just like a man, where her ball landed when it became hidden in autumn leaves. Why, it went right in the middle of the fairway—about forty yards farther than she usually drives it. What a great shot! With the spirit of an athlete, a male athlete, she does not bother looking for the lost ball...you know, avoid slow play...and so she drops that ball without penalty. (Why should she be penalized for having such a generous and considerate spirit?)

This kind of fair and fast play results in the woman's game getting better and better; in fact, women who have played with men often during the year generally will consistently beat them by now. Women who have played with other women all year will also play better by fall. Yet it is unlikely their scores will improve as much as those of the coed players have.

By fall women are recording their best scores. This is not when they make their best shots, however. Their best shots are in winter, when they cannot make any shots at all.

Winter

In winter, women golfers who live up north have much lower handicaps than their female counterparts down south. Of course, they cannot play golf up north during the winter, but they can remember how they did play—and they played very, very well.

These golfers do not want to lose their skills, so they set up programs to keep their superior golf skills in place. Some engage in creative visualization. They remember the best shots they ever made—again and again. They remember them so often that, in their mind, the shots become run-of-the mill, just their ordinary shots. So, as the winter goes by, these lady golfers become better and better players, and they stay that way—until spring.

Others, of a less metaphysical orientation, visit indoor driving ranges. Indoor driving ranges are great. Imagine the ball you just hit 10 yards to the right side of the net flying 210 yards straight down the middle of the fairway. Every woman golfer imagines accordingly. "If only, if only, I could have hit that one outside...."

Of course, even in the snow belt, women golfers do hit the sticks outside during the winter on occasion. That is usually on a winter golfing trip to the Caribbean or Mexico. What happens if you don't play well there? Just blame it on the two feet of snow that kept you off the course back home. Of course, if you do play well...can you imagine how well you would have played if you were in practice?

Women in warm places take advantage of the weather. They take classes to "get the edge" on the upcoming spring tournaments and league play. Women golfers like to take golf lessons. They usually take these classes with friends they have invited to join them. These are the same friends they hope to beat the socks off in their upcoming tournament and league play.

Whether they live in the North or the South, women golfers do not get to play as much as they want during winter, partially because they are preparing for the winter holidays. Women golfers enjoy Christmas more than their nongolfing friends, and they are such clever shoppers.

Women golfers are almost clairvoyant in their choice of gifts for friends. Let's see…a golf figurine for Lisa, a golf ornament for Anne, a golf key chain for Mary, a golf glove for Terry, a golf calendar for Vicki, a golf outing for Janice, and a golf shoe-cleaning kit for Kay. Everyone got something they wanted—something connected to golf! Women golfers make the best friends. They truly understand the deepest desires of their companions, and they are not afraid of showing some creativity.

Cocktail-Napkin Wisdom

First (Long Island Iced) Tee: A napkin with a picture of two women golfing. One says to the other, "I'd like to lower my handicap. Let's play men's rules today."

Second (Long Island Iced) Tee: A napkin with a picture of a twister chasing two women golfers. One says to the other, "Looks like another Texas scramble!"

Third (Long Island Iced) Tee: A napkin with a picture of an older, middle-aged, and young woman. "The three wise women: your attorney, mother, and golf pro."

"I'd like to lower my handicap, let's play men's rules today."

Fourth (Long Island Iced)Tee: A napkin with a nun hitting a driver. "I am not a hooker."

Fifth (Long Island Iced) Tee: A napkin with a picture of a beautiful golf course. "The fairer sex fares best on the fairways."

Sixth (Long Island Iced) Tee: A napkin with two women at a golf course talking about a man golfer they are playing with. "When he said he shot in the seventies, I didn't know he was talking about the front nine."

Seventh (Long Island Iced) Tee: A napkin with two women golfers running from an alligator. "I'm tired of these Florida scrambles."

Eighth (Long Island Iced) Tee: A napkin with two women golfers sitting in a golf cart, looking unhappily at their golf scores on the eighteenth hole. "Let's improve our game the way men do. Where is the eraser?"

Ninth (Long Island Iced) Tee: A napkin depicting a country club's memo that reads: "This club is a firm supporter of equal opportunity for all male golfers."

Eighth Hole

Women Play Business Golf

Getting Corporate Approval for the Gentlemen-Only Game

I once golfed with a man who told me the name of golf was derived from a very old sign in an even older Scottish clubhouse, "Gentlemen Only, Ladies Forbidden." I think he was mistaken. I think he must have gotten it mixed up with a business golf outing.

Business golf is the ultimate perquisite. It is an afternoon off without using vacation time. It is $125 greens fees on the company credit card. It is a feeling of power, a feeling of importance, a feeling of enrichment. You are, after all, playing on the company's dime.

There is something special about golfing during business hours. No matter how poorly you play, someone in your foursome will always remind you, "Hey, it's better than being in the office." Now ain't that the truth! Today the grass seems a little greener and the fairways a little fairer.

The only downside to business golf is that for most of us there isn't any. Very few men and even fewer women get to play business golf. Marketing and sales representatives occasionally do. For paper pushers and number crunchers, however, it is a once-in-every-five-years event. This is because business golf is a very exclusive activity. If it were otherwise, it could result in public disclosure of a highly confidential trade secret—namely, that business golf is fun. (Oops!)

Men especially are interested in keeping this secret. They play the martyr before and after a game of business golf. "Business golf is not fun; it is work; it is hard work; it's tough to entertain those clients," they whine as they each turn in their $275 single-afternoon entertainment expenses.

Women who play business golf are always elated. They do not act that way, though. It is much more professional to complain as you get ready to exchange your briefcase for your golf bag. "I just don't know what I am going to do," the female attorney tells her partner. "I have this sixty-page brief to read and these boring interrogatories to answer, but Mr. Big Client wants to go golfing. I'm just going to have to give this paperwork to our new associate to handle."

Professions that serve clients are natural fits for business-golf opportunities. Many firms, however, require a woman golfer to prove her golfing ability before turning her loose on a client.

"So," your boss says, "You want to take Clyde Client out

golfing. I didn't even realize you golfed. How long have you been playing?"

"Fifteen years," you lie.

"Then it sounds like a good idea. But before you take him out, why don't we go out first?" he asks you.

"Great!" you respond.

Your boss looks at his calendar. "How about one o'clock on a Wednesday...in June...say, two years from now?"

Unfortunately, there is just one thing more difficult in this world than a man hitting a straight drive. That, of course, is a woman getting her firm to pick up greens fees. It is not because men don't like women. It's just because men think women will lose more clients on the course than men lose balls.

Once you understand that, you really can see their point. That would be, after all, one heck of a lot of clients.

Playing a Round With Clients

Women never should play around with clients when inviting them to play a round. Golf is not like sex. It is nothing to joke about.

Men take golf seriously. Men clients like playing with women, particularly women who pay. Women clients also love to share their sport with business contacts, especially if that contact is someone who hits from the same tees they do.

Golfing with clients is different from golfing with members

of your club or with strangers at a municipal course. The golfers who belong to your club are stuck with you for as long as you pay your dues. The golfers at the muni show up at seven o'clock in the morning for the privilege of being paired up blindly with someone—you—at eleven. They may not think you are the perfect partner, but your only link is the links anyway. Compare these people to your clients. Your clients lead you to wealth much as fairways lead you to greens. Your clients determine where you can afford to live, what you can afford to eat, and whether (gulp) you can afford to play golf.

When you golf with your clients, everything counts...the impression you create, the course you select to play on...why, even the actual number of hits you take! There is no doubt that playing a round with a client will affect your career. Let's just hope you end on the upswing and do not shank your shot. Successful golfing with your clients requires a very special set of skills.

First, you need confidence.   You must be able to play well, even if you are not playing the game well. You must enjoy yourself and give your client the opportunity to enjoy himself. All golfers enjoy themselves after they have eagled a hole. You have to enjoy yourself after you finish the hole on which you whiffed, sliced, and lost a ball, too.

Why? Your potential client will never hire you as a management consultant if you start shouting, "You idiot! You idiot!" every

"I'll consider this a good year if I can get a commercial for the Dinah Shore Nabisco Tournament."

time your ball makes its predictable slice. OK, maybe you are a lousy driver. Don't compound it by also admitting you are an idiot.

Your client also will never give your firm a vendor contract if you spend the day telling him you play much better when you are not playing with him. "Hmmm," he will think. "Maybe you will have the same type of excuse when your company does not meet its orders."

Show off your high self-esteem. Laugh off your bad shots. There is only one failure in business golf, and that is not getting the business. No one expects you to make an ace, too.

Second, you must exercise control. If your client gets a double bogey on a hole, don't scream for joy when you birdie it. On the other hand, play up all of your client's successes. If he or she scores a par or birdie, butter him up. "Competition is tough today. Are you sure your handicap is a 25? Looks as if you are playing more like someone in the teens."

Most important, never, ever act like a man. Even a man should not act like a man. No matter how poorly you are playing, do not throw your sticks. There is only one thing more difficult to explain to your boss than why you didn't land the contract. That is how your clubs landed on your client's head.

Third, you must exercise client strategy as well as course strategy. The most successful business deals are made at the nineteenth hole. Don't try to make them while your client is putting for par. It will only give your client something new to blame for her three putts—you! Business talk on the course has gone the way of metal-spiked shoes. Leave both behind in the locker room.

Fourth, you must have the courage to be yourself. Don't be afraid to be a good, positive, fun-loving, considerate golfer. In other words, be yourself—a woman golfer.

Fifth, you must be able to play the game. Forget this stuff about golf being an equalizer. Whoever said golf was a great equalizer was obviously playing with someone within twenty strokes of his or her handicap on a Saturday afternoon at a public golf course.

There are certain business repercussions associated with how you golf. These mainly fall into the following five scenarios.

Possible Outcomes

You lose big with a female client. If you shoot twenty strokes more than your female client, she will think you are a poor golfer. If your boss asks how you played, she will report how you scored. You will be equalized. You will feel no better or worse than anyone else in the unemployment line.

You lose big with a male client. If you shoot twenty strokes more than your male client, he will not tell your boss that you played poorly. He will just say that you played like a typical woman. You won't be fired. You just never will be authorized to golf with a client again. You will be equalized, however. You will be equal to a caddie who doesn't carry bags and can't estimate distance.

You barely beat your client, or your client barely beats you. If you shoot five strokes less than your client, he or she will say you are a good golfer. Good golfers make good business deals. You may land your firm a new contract and yourself a small raise.

If you shoot five strokes more than your client, he or she will say you are a great golfer. Great golfers make great business deals. You will land your firm a new contract and yourself a big raise.

You kill your female client. If you shoot twenty strokes less than your female client, she will tell you and everyone you know that you are absolutely great. This is particularly the case if you tell her that when you had played only for the length of time she has, you always scored at least ten points higher than she does. Play that hot and your career will be hotter. More than your ball will land on green. Your bank account will see plenty of green as well.

You kill your male client. If you shoot twenty strokes less than your male client, he will encourage you to quit your job and become a pro. After all, he does not want to play golf with you ever again anyway.

Playing a Round With Colleagues

People who don't mix business with pleasure seldom get much of either. Men may go west to get ahead, but we women go golfing.

"She's a great new account exec—but whatever you do don't let her play against any of her clients. She never loses."

Most of us, after all, can derive a lot more success out of our drives than distance. We also can use golf to improve our working relationships with our colleagues.

Golfing with colleagues is like having lunch with the boss. It is just a good thing to do once in a while. It is great to be in good social standing with the people in the office. It also makes business a little more personal. This makes people less apt to do mean things to you and tell you not to take them personally.

There are, of course, options other than golf. You could ask a colleague, for instance, to join you for a drink. When you drink a round with a colleague, the impact on your working relationship lasts as long as the alcohol in your systems. If you play a round with a colleague, however, your working relationship will forever more be greens struck.

No wonder we women don't golf just with the people we have lunch with every day! While it is wonderful to play with male supporters, a businesswoman golfer also sometimes will put together unusual foursomes. Maybe she will include the colleague she wishes was not, the guy at work who is trying to steal her job, and the woman whose support is crucial to the success of her unsuccessful department. In other words, a woman does not golf only with friends. She golfs with people who *should* be friends as well.

"Should be" the friends are a little like sand traps. Remember the reaction you had last time your ball landed in a trap? "Why, oh why," you thought, "did I ever make a New Year's resolution to give up swearing?" After you made a sandie, however, you remembered. Sand can be your friend.

Likewise, when the average woman golfer meets an obstacle maker on the job, she does not spend her time plotting and scheming how to get around him or her. That would take too much time away from her golf. No, she turns her obstacle makers into her personal par makers.

How? She learns to make her strokes work for her. She uses the golf experience to build teamwork. She becomes as tight with her colleagues as recruits in the last week of boot camp. Wow! She actually begins to like them!

When you and your colleagues share an afternoon together for the sole purpose of whacking a ball as few times as possible, teamwork becomes second nature to each of you. You have already joined your minds, money, and mulligans for the greater purpose of golf. Why should business get in the way of your friendship?

When you have golfed with your colleagues, you each have seen the other fail miserably. He saw you hit a ball into the water when faced with a three-foot-wide ditch. You would have been better off if you had just left your ball in your pocket and jumped across. You saw him score an eight on a par-3, eighteen-handicap hole. He would have been better off if he had just thrown his ball.

You also, however, saw each other's successes. You remember

how he parred the number-one-handicap hole on the most difficult course in town. He is still amazed that you shot a birdie on the signature hole on that resort course.

You have seen more than the actions of each other's ball. You have seen each other's reactions. When you golf with someone, you learn a lot about them—important stuff. Not just whether they tan or burn or whether they drag their heels on the greens. You learn stuff that applies even under fluorescent office lights.

For instance, if you golf with someone who is hot tempered and throws his clubs, you learn not to tell him bad news right before an important meeting. You also learn not to ask him golfing again. Once you play with the eternal optimist who always thinks his next shot will be better, you understand why he is so successful in the business world. You watch how his mental discipline affects his course—and career—strategy. You mimic his attempts to stay positive. You also learn to consult him before you see your chiropractor or astrologer when you need an attitude adjustment.

When you play with the smart golfer who always takes the high-percentage shots, you understand why he never backs your speculative projects. Finally, you learn that the impulsive player who would rather take a stroke than give up the chance of hitting a career shot would rather you keep your bear-market news to yourself and your broker.

Your colleagues also learn about you. How wonderful! After

all, women golfers are much more pleasant to play with than men. It is thus just a gimme that you have given your colleagues more than a few putts. You also have driven one heck of a great impression.

Men Talk Better Golf Than Women

If you want to move and shake in the $200,000-per-year executive community, you must successfully navigate certain rites of passage. For instance, your credentials should include the ability to:

- Give a speech without being the least bit nervous
- Order a bottle of high-quality wine without looking at the price list to determine which wine is of the best quality
- Eat a baked, stuffed lobster without asking anyone how to get the meat out of the claws
- Steal a colleague's paper and take the credit for it so gracefully that she thanks you for giving her the exposure
- Talk golf

No, I did not say play golf. I said talk golf. Talking golf requires a lot more skill than playing it. For instance, if you want to play at Pebble Beach Golf Links, you call up the pro shop and get a tee time. After paying $225, "Fore!" You are on the course, playing golf.

Ask yourself, though, how you are going to talk about this

game with others. How will you tell your colleagues, your clients, and other people you want to impress that you played this course?

If you are like most women, you know it is a serious breach of corporate etiquette to stop by the office of the chairman of the board of directors to shout, "Guess what! I spent my bonus this year on a trip to California so I can play the course you took all of our top sales representatives to last year!" This conduct not only is unbecoming, it also can be very distracting if you barge in just when he is about to putt on one of those practice mats in his office.

Most women, though, do not tell the story so that they will make the right impression. As a result, most men think of women as playing at golf rather than golfing. Did you ever play golf with a male colleague with whom you talked about golf at least once a week for several months before you got together on the course? You go out and shoot nine strokes over your handicap and twelve strokes more than he does. What does he say about you to his buddies back at the office? "Wow, she really does play golf. It was almost like playing with a man."

What would have happened if you won? He just would have explained, "Golf is the only game I do not excel in. You see, I am extremely athletic. Golf, however, is a skill, rather than an athletic game. That's why I am not a scratch golfer. To play golf well, you have to play a lot. I am just too important to get away from the office that much."

The truth of the matter is that we women may play a good game, but men talk better golf than we do. Their golf networks have more web and fewer holes to fall through than ours. That's because men golfers talk up their game and talk down their handicaps while women golfers tend to be humble—even truthful—about their games. Men golfers are thus more successful in creating successful impressions. They are even adept in the art of dropping names of hard-to-get-on private courses or megabuck public courses. It is as natural to them as taking a mulligan after hitting a poor drive.

A man golfer who just came back from a trip to California, for instance, may humbly say to his boss, a regional sales manager, over lunch, "Boy, my handicap just went up a point or two this weekend. I had a couple of tough rounds of golf."

"Oh, really, what did you shoot?" asks his boss.

"An 86. Six points over my handicap!" he lies.

"Wow! You must have a pretty good handicap. What is it? An 8?"

"Well, it was," he lies. "I don't know what it will be now, though." He chuckles. "Of course, I wasn't playing at my club. This course was pretty tough."

"Oh, where did you play?"

"At Pebble Beach," he replies casually.

"Well, if you shot an 86 there, we'll have to get you signed up to play at our meeting out there next year. Probably impress the hell out of our vice president for sales."

"Oh, yeah...that would be great." He casually yawns.

He is invited. The man spends the next year attending golf schools and practicing his game. He then attends the Pebble Beach Golf Outing. He scores exactly what he really shot the year before—108. He posts his score and sits down and has a couple of beers. He even stops by the table where his boss and the vice president for sales are sitting and shares a few golf jokes. Eventually, the regional sales manager and the VP–Sales review the scores to determine who won their tournament. The VP–Sales turns to the regional manager in amazement. He is shocked at this man's score. After all, the regional manager had shared his discussion with the golfer about his game at Pebble Beach last year.

"No wonder he is such a good golfer. Even when he has a bad day and really blows it, he just blows it off."

"Yeah, that boy has real potential," responds the regional sales manager.

Now consider what happens to the woman who invites that same regional manager to lunch and decides to engage in a similar discussion. "What a weekend! I did get some R&R on the golf course, but I bet my handicap went up at least one or two strokes."

"You have a handicap? What is it?" the manager asks her.

"It's a 27," she confesses.

"Nothing wrong with that!" he says. "In fact, it's in the same range as mine. Enough small talk, though. How is that new project coming along?"

Women Business Golfers Have More Fun Than Men

Men business golfers spend their time on the course making an impression. They want to look good, play great, and move ahead. They want to beat this person. They want to lose gracefully to that person. No, no, not to the client. To the scratch golfer they got stuck playing with.

Men see business golf as an opportunity—an opportunity to show their stuff. Women business golfers, on the other hand, play a very different game. They just play golf.

Like men, women business golfers, of course, realize a good round of golf may lead to a better round of contracts or to a promotion later. Unlike her male counterpart, however, a woman invited by a client or colleague to play golf knows she is already winning. If she weren't, she would not have been invited.

Most men do not invite women to golf. Every man a woman meets assumes she does not play golf. Those who discover that she does assume she does not play well, or, at least, well enough to play with them.

The man who thus invites a woman golfing is an exceptional

man. He is not like other men. For one thing, his self-esteem is higher than the average drainage ditch. For another, he likes doing business with women.

Unlike a man, then, when a woman business golfer is invited golfing she does not have to worry about appeasing egos and playing politics. She does not have to blow her game because her partner has blown his. When she is on the course, she can just play her game. She thus gets to play golf, while most men feel as if they have to work at it.

Consider how each handles a lost ball. The woman will just drop another one after a moment's search. The businessman, however, is about as willing to do that as he is to let someone else sit next to the boss at this year's Christmas party. No, a ten-minute search is required. Not a second less.

Likewise, a woman playing golf is concerned with the quality of the time spent. A man working at golf is obsessed with his score. At the midway point between the ninth and tenth holes, the woman will ask the other members of her foursome if they want a hot dog. The man will ask his playing partners what their scores are.

One of the reasons businessmen and women have such different approaches to the game is that they have such different expectations. Assume ten men and ten women attend a business meeting that includes an afternoon of golf. All of them plan on hitting the sticks.

The women golfers expect one heck of a good time. The men

golfers expect to win—the game, the business, and the respect of everyone there. Women business golfers have fun; men business golfers have ulcers.

The Toughest Obstacle in Business Golf: The Men-Only Grill

Women go to golf schools and learn how to get out of sand, over water, through grass, and around trees. There is one obstacle, however, even a pro can't teach you how to overcome—the men-only grill.

Surprise! The men-only grill still exists at many courses today. Women golfers continue to be shocked to discover that there are country clubs where women are barred from eating a hamburger next to a man. After all, they took up golf to play with their business associates. It is thus only fair for women to be able to go to the nineteenth hole with them afterward to close deals and open beers.

The ideology of "fair," however, is a subject for discussions of handicap indexes and course design. "Associate membership" is the buzzword at many golf courses.

As a rule, business golf is played at the priciest clubs around. These clubs have been designed for people with discriminating taste—many of whom discriminate against women.

The only thing funny about this form of discrimination is the fact that in many states it still is legal. For some reason, the right to buy a burger and swing a club on Saturday morning has not been embraced within the concept of equal opportunity.

Of course, there are a lot of things you can do about it. Call your congresswoman. Call your senator. Demand equality. While you are waiting for legislative action, however, you had better plan on eating your business lunches elsewhere. Trust me. Even your supportive male associates will not want to walk into a men-only grill for a bite to eat after eighteen holes in the company of a woman with whom they have just played golf. That will be true even if they are hungry and even if you are playing at your club, not theirs.

The problem may be, however, that unless you draw the men's attention to the fact that the men-only grill is, in fact, for men only, they may not even notice it. Don't blame them. It is not their fault. They look around, see only men, and then look for earrings. "Let's see," the average heterosexual man subconsciously reasons. "It doesn't look like a gay bar." Men may be blind to discrimination while women are blinded by it.

Successful business golf requires you to sidestep such differences. It is improper business etiquette to ask your male client to wage your war against inequality. It would be like asking him to burn your bra.

The successful businesswoman cannot require her golf partner to agitate against inequality. She must instead create a world—let's call it Wallina's World—that is a business world with equality.

She cannot lose her client to the men-only grill, so she picks a neutral meeting spot for beer and pretzels and the opportunity to win his company's wallet.

"Let's meet at Birdie's after we change out of our golf shoes. You'll just love it there! It's got the best hot dogs in town!" she says to her male client as they head in from the eighteenth hole.

If he says he'd rather go to Bogie's, the men-only grill, she turns him down as gently as a two-inch putt. "Oh, sorry, but that is the men-only grill. Let's go to Birdie's instead. It has better atmosphere anyway."

Women can, of course, avoid these issues by playing only at those clubs that do not have men-only grills. So say the discriminating men who voted on the bylaws that do not allow women to chow down next to them. The better solution would be for all clubs to voluntarily open up their grills to members of both sexes. This is, however, about as likely as a beginner golfer having a hook.

Ninth Hole

The Romantic Side of the Game

The Couple Who Plays Together Stays Together

Golf is the best marriage counselor. Consider the couple who goes to a therapist. They pay one hundred dollars for a fifty-minute-hour session. During that time, they sit on a couch in a stuffy office on a Saturday afternoon. Each discusses why the other is not meeting his or her expectations.

"He doesn't help with the dishes. He makes snide remarks at parties. He doesn't care about me at all," says the nagging wife.

"Well, maybe you should stop sniping at me," says the mean husband.

"Whose fault do you think it is?" the wife asks the therapist.

"You'll each have to decide that for yourself," answers the wise and rich therapist.

Compare this to what happens to couples who go golfing.

They pay one hundred dollars for their greens fees. They get fresh air, sunshine, and some exercise. They don't talk about the kids, the roof leaking, and the housekeeper quitting. They don't mentally rehearse each other's lines from the party they went to the night before. They are not acting out some melodrama through their children. They are, instead, in touch with their own inner child.

Why, they are golfing! The game absorbs them completely, releasing them from life's little problems, yet it makes them work together as each keeps track of the other's balls.

They do not play this game for a mere fifty-minute hour, either. They are together for at least four-and-a-half hours. In fact, most married couples find that by the nineteenth hole they feel the same way about their spouse as they do about other golfers. They like them.

Their spouse, they discover, is the kind of person with whom they want to spend another hour, having a drink inside the clubhouse, and then spend a lifetime enjoying the game.

This does not mean that playing golf is a game of marital bliss. There may be some very tough times during those eighteen holes. Yet golf is great practice for marriage. This is not only because it is easier to wear a wedding ring than it is to swing a club. Golf is tougher than marriage because, unlike marriage, golf truly is a game of "for better or for worse." In golf, you can't quit playing with your partner just because he does not meet your expectations.

Let's say your partner meditates for ten minutes over his ball before swinging, or he has a tendency to talk just as you are about to take a swing, or he doesn't fix the green when his ball lands there. In golf, you must convince him to change his behavior without threatening to dump him on the next hole. Furthermore, on the golf course, it is politically incorrect to attribute any golfer's poor golfing habits, including your husband's, to a basic inability to give or accept love.

This downside is offset, however, by the considerable upside of having a golf-course location. Here, the other members of your foursome will gladly jump in to offer their opinion on any breach-of-etiquette issue that you would like to discuss. Unlike a therapist, they also will gladly assign blame to whomever they perceive as the responsible party.

In fact, golf is such good therapy that married couples who play together have very happy marriages. That is why married couples make the best partners. That is, they make the best partners for Sunday afternoon play. Married couples make very poor partners in tough twosome tournaments. That is why alternate-ball games are called divorce golf. Married couples also make very poor partners on Saturday mornings or Wednesday afternoons. That's when everyone is serious about his or her game. Married golfers make the best partners in casual games of golf. Those are the games where no one intends to turn in a handicap unless they do particularly well or particularly poorly, depending on their upward or downward handicap goal.

"It all started in high school when I asked if I could carry
her books home from class."

Golfers married to each other are very visible on the course. Other golfers can tell a lot about how much "for better or for worse" a couple's life is when they watch them play together.

Men and women golfers with a sense of unity really support each other as they play. If, for instance, the woman's ball lands in the sand, her husband is right behind her with a rake in hand. He'll do the yard work when she steps out. If her husband hits his ball 170 yards into a water hazard, the happy wife shakes her head in wonder. "Boy, you don't even get rewarded for your good shots on this course."

The couple in love begin their golf game like an act of love. They are gentle but not too slow; they are considerate of each other's feelings; and they don't give each other too much coaching as each gradually seduces the other into fulfilling powerful, positive expectations.

Happily married couples are the masters of the mental side of the game. They excel at bringing out the best in each other's game. They salute each other's good shots and diminish the importance (or even the number, when recording) of the bad ones.

Happily married golfers also extend their lives and games to include other golfers in their circle. They often will take weekend trips with other players. Their destinations will be sunny resorts with early tee times, afternoon pool parties, and evening entertainment. These golfing excursions improve their games and enhance relationships, though usually relationships with the couple's friends rather than with each other. Couples who play together generally prefer to have female and male twosomes in the golf carts. Part of the reason for this is that men and women usually play from different tees, so it is logistically preferable. Another reason is that happily married golfers understand why they are happy. They each give the other enough space so that their mate can hit the inevitable bad shot, and they won't be the one who will loudly announce to the world, "Fore!"

A Golf-Course Romance

Single women like to meet available men with attractive traits. There are a lot of men on the golf course. Thus, a small number of single women actually take up golf for the sole purpose of meeting men.

These are women who do not yet realize that getting an unknown man to play golf with them is more difficult than getting Don Juan to commit to marriage. They think that golf-course romances bloom like wildflowers. What they don't realize is that the results generally resemble allergic reactions.

Some women actually have met their beloved on a patch of Bermuda grass. One would think, given the pair's mutual interest in the game, that such romances would be up to par. A golf-course romance, however, won't help you get out of the bunker. Obstacles abound in this sand trap of passion.

The first issue that must be resolved by two golfing partners turned intimate is where they should play on Saturday mornings. Both the man and the woman want to play. Maybe one of them, though, belongs to a club where only men are allowed to play on Saturday mornings. (Gee, you wonder—which one?) Rest assured that neither belongs to a club where only women can play on Saturday morning.

Maybe the man's favorite course is not the same as the woman's. After all, just because a hole is great from the white tees doesn't necessarily mean it is great when you tee off from the red tees. It can be daunting to have the demanding obstacle that is the course signature located a scant five yards in front of your tee box.

Even if the two lovers agree about where they like to play, however, they also must consider if they will play together. No golfer is going to be happy dating another golfer who leaves him or her alone every Saturday morning—every golfer's prime time. Yet the new couple must confront the fact that each of them already has an established foursome—and their new partner isn't part of that group. Golfers don't take their regular foursomes lightly. A man who talks all day long about his fear of commitment is totally committed to his Saturday-morning regulars. A woman is, too.

If the two romancing golfers are lucky, they both have a standard Saturday foursome. If only one of them has a standard Saturday foursome, they could be rescued by one of these regulars breaking an arm or leg and being unable to play. In that case, the romance partner actually would be welcome to join the foursome.

The other issue—too embarrassing even for pillow talk for two new lovers—is that maybe, just maybe, one member of the couple does not really enjoy playing golf with the other. He or she may prefer playing golf with a complete stranger at a municipal course who carries his cigarette pack rolled up in the sleeve of a collarless tee shirt so that he can show off his tattoo of a rolling golf ball when he flexes his muscles. You can bet that if the man doesn't want to play with the woman it is because he believes the love of his life just doesn't swing fast or far enough to challenge him. On the other hand, if the woman doesn't want to golf with the man, it is because she really would rather get her tips from a pro than from someone who shoots six more strokes than she does even though his score reflects fourteen fewer.

This kind of golf-course management is just the tip of the bunker for problems of the romancing golf-course couple, however. Certain types of behavior, which may be well accepted elsewhere, simply are not tolerated on the golf course. For instance, while throwing clubs may be optional, throwing an admiring look at your cart mate after a poor shot is not. After all, golf is not a date; it is a game, and a damn serious one to every golfer who is playing well.

No, sirree; flirty conduct is not proper golf etiquette. The one and only exception to this is the common local rule that allows men golfers who are under 120 in age or score to flirt with the attractive female college student who works as a beverage-cart driver.

All romances have their unexpected twists, but golfing romances have more than their fair share of doglegs. It is tough to get away from everything when you are bringing everything, namely him, to the golf course. While all men critique—I mean help—the women golfers they play with, it can be tough for the woman golfer to accept her lover's words of guidance without wondering if the relationship is destroying the one long-lasting love of her life: golf.

A golf-course romance won't get you out of the bunker. Many of the available men on the golf course are available for a reason…their wives are out of town. One of them may try to woo you with unusually courteous conduct, such as actually waiting for you to hit your ball from the red tees before going in search of the ball(s) which he just drove. However, a simple demonstration of proper golf etiquette does not mean that this is the man for you.

Nonetheless, I am sure some of you ladies will search the course for your own beloved (that is, the one in addition to your golf ball). It will be helpful to you to know how to recognize that the wild and zany way you hook has hooked a man. Listen to the man who says at the end of your game, "Thanks for the game. You can play golf with me anytime."

Of course, the reason he says this isn't because he is looking for a partner for Saturday mornings. It is a flirtatious statement that has brought him off-the-course success previously when he has used it on the course with other women. It is meant to be a compliment, to show that even though you are a woman, you can play with him, a man. It is the highest form of flattery from a man golfer.

You might respond, "I'd be happy to play with you again some time. I just hope you might speed it up a little next time." If he laughs, marry him. If he turns green, suggest that he use the red tees next time and then thank your lucky balls that you will never have to play with him again.

Your Significant Other As Your Caddie

Caddies have gone the way of wooden woods. The average golfer today never has had a caddie Some clubs do allow competitors in important tournaments to use one, though. The catch, of course, is that you must provide your own.

Most women like the idea of having a caddie. How wonderful! Caddies, after all, are an excellent support system. The caddie's job is to take care of your clubs and to keep those chips from falling off your shoulder after you hit a slice.

A woman golfer usually asks her significant other to caddie for her. After all, she figures, he is always watching my game. He gives me tips all the time. Who better could help me with club selection, estimating distance, and managing my emotions during a competition?

About a quarter of the women who think this way are correct. These women have mates or dates who take an active interest in their games. The problem is that half of these men also take an active interest in their competitors' games, too. "You're lifting up during the swing. That's why you keep topping your balls," your husband tells your opponent, who thus far has the same score you have.

The other half of the men in this top percentile do remain loyal to the women they accompany. "She's not playing much better than you, honey," your boyfriend says. "All you have to do is birdie the next six holes and you can make up for the thirteen you got on the last one."

The remaining 75 percent of male caddies are not as supportive. These men become bored after the second hole. By then, they have realized what it is like to be on the course for four or five hours and not hit a single ball themselves. However, they do try to remain cheerful during the process. "Oh well, at least I am getting some fresh air and exercise," the average man consoles himself as he drives down the cart path, smoking a cigar.

All men caddies use carts whenever allowed. After all, those bags get heavy. Three-quarters of the men also use them so that they will have a place to sit when their wives are about to putt for a birdie or par.

Women have fired their husband caddies for doing that, but the average woman does not object. It may not seem comforting having your husband ask you, "How did you do?" right after you drove, because he wasn't looking. He is still better company, though, than your women competitors, who *were* looking but chose to say nothing about the best shot of your career.

A woman who is using her significant other as a caddie has more to worry about than how the business side of their relationship is working out, anyway. She has her game to consider. Tournaments that require caddies always have great prizes. She could get a parking space, or a set of clubs, or a gift certificate from a pro shop.

She and her husband are sitting in their cart waiting for the foursome in front of them to finish putting. She starts daydreaming. "If I won, what would I get from that pro shop?"

Her husband interrupts her. "Boy, these women sure play slow."

"Women golfers don't play slow," she responds automatically. Then she decides. "Ahh...I know what I can get. Something I really could use. In fact, I could use it right now. If I win, I'll get an electronic caddie!"

Hitting the Sticks in Cancún

Caribbean vacations are made for lovers. Ahh...the sun...the sea ...the sand...the sand traps. The Caribbean is a golf lover's paradise —and not too bad a place to bring a spouse, either.

Golfers visit tropical resort locations to break away from the stress and monotony of everyday life. Who cares whether a mutual fund goes up or down five cents, when you have a bigger problem on your mind—namely, the man you love is five strokes, and one Bahama Mama, ahead of you? Who cares if the local yokels in the states want to condemn your retirement property and put a freeway through it, when your ball just landed on an iguana's back? Who cares if everyone you work with is a jerk, if the couple you were just paired up with are even jerkier?

Hitting the sticks in Cancún is the surest way to hit into any golfer's heart. Married couples love golf vacations and love each other just a little bit more when they are on one. As they partner up with their life's partner, they share more than eighteen holes. Golf is, after all, a lot like life…the dreams and divots…the bad bounces and good outs…the lucky birdies and the undeserved bogeys…the obstacles and the opportunities…and the absolutely unexpected dogleg.

"A lot of people misread greens, but misreading a golf map," he exclaims, "must be a first!"

"Laugh all you want," she says. "I am. After all, I have plenty of room for error. Right now I'm winning by three strokes net."

There is more than room for error on a resort course, of course. There also is plenty of time for it. Resort golfers are slow golfers. Resort golfers think nothing of taking the same shot six or seven times until they finally clear that water hazard so their spouse, who is using a camcorder, can capture it. "Yep, it's a tough little hole," he tells his friends back home after hefty editing, "but you can't really tell from the video. It's just not the same as being there." Well, it certainly is not the same for the couple behind him.

When you are hitting your sticks on the islands with the one you love, rather than playing golf at home, you appreciate the pauses. They give you more time to breathe in the salty air and to taste the salty ring around your husband's margarita. They give you more time to enjoy each other and the spiritual pleasure of being.

Of course, a golf vacation to Cancún does not have the legendary quality a trip to Scotland would have. You don't take a piece of history home in your hearts when you are playing golf in the Caribbean. In fact, your heart does not even have the room for it. It is too elated with the present moment to be cluttered up with antiques.

When you golf in Cancún, you golf in Cancún. No other place or time exists but that moment—or moments—or hour or so—as you wait for those slowpokes to tee off in front of you. Time is irrelevant. Heck! If you were smart enough to get one of those all-inclusive deals, every hour is happy hour anyway. So what's the rush?

It will be your turn eventually, and when it is you will be

ready. That is, you will be ready as soon as you find your camcorder.

Birdies Are the Best Fore!play

Some people say power is an aphrodisiac. We golfers know it is.

How alluring to hit a ball from here to forever (or at least 180 yards)! How intriguing to share someone's hole in one. The most romantic move of all, however, is making a birdie with the man you love.

Birdies are the best fore!play. When you shoot a birdie, not only do you feel good about your game, the world feels good about you. Shooting a birdie is like finding the bluebird of happiness on your shoulder and then seeing that this time the only souvenir left is a merry chirp.

How wonderful it is to play golf—and play golf well—with your beloved. It means your union has been blessed by the golf gods. It means you two are psychologically well suited to each other. Your stress-free, made-in-heaven-for-at-least-the-greens marriage has created the perfect environment for love and success. Yes! Yes! You love golf and your husband!

A woman who scores a birdie looks at her marriage ring a little differently. It is not some primitive symbol of bondage or ownership or belonging. It is a link. It is her link to the links. It is a sign of a stay-until-you-die or at least until-you-triple-bogey relationship.

After you hit a birdie with the one you love, you just can't help realizing how lucky you are. Your husband is your lucky charm. How many women golfers actually can say that? For that matter, how many women golfers can say much of anything, with their husbands always giving them advice? Compare that with what you get from your husband—his unqualified admiration.

No other man ever could take your husband's place. You have scored one-under-par with him. It is the ultimate conquest. You've driven a long way, baby, on this hole, and you have the golf and marital scores to prove it.

Making a birdie is the best fore!play. It also is not bad for your score.

Why Breaking 90 May Be Harder Than Breaking Up

A lot more than just golf makes this world go round. There are relationships, for example.

Women have relationships with their mothers, their fathers, their friends, their siblings, their children. They also have "a Relationship." A Relationship is a very, very important relationship. A women in a Relationship may, for instance, even return His phone call before she returns the phone call of her best friend who has a Saturday morning tee time.

A woman in a Relationship defines herself by it. "No, I can't go out with the girls on Friday anymore. I'm in a Relationship now."

In some ways, a Relationship is like golf. You can learn golf in one year or thirty; a Relationship also takes varying amounts of time to cultivate. It takes at least one Friday night. A woman in a Relationship is like a woman who golfs; she is committed—some even may say addicted—to predicting the outcome. She may pretend she does not care very much about him. She may not even call him. A woman also will pretend she does not care very much about her score. She may not bother adding it up after the front nine. That is just a pretense, however. She does care—very, very much.

In fact, a Relationship is so important that women do not like to rush into breaking one up. They ease into breaking it up the same way men think women also approach golf—very, very slowly.

A woman about to end a Relationship first consults with her inner circle—that is, her friends, her very best friends—maybe 23 or 26 of them. She will tell them why she is thinking about calling it quits: "He doesn't make me feel special." "He's obsessed with his work." "I feel as if I'm competing with his ex-wife." "I'm just bored with him." It is not enough to tell them just once. It takes about six months of gut-wrenching dialogues before she finally is ready to stop. That is, it takes that long before she is ready to stop defending Him after her friends agree with all of the bad things she says about Him.

After this mental preparation comes rehearsal. Should she say

"Let's be friends" at the beginning or the end of their discussion? Should she say it in person or on the phone? Should they be at their favorite restaurant or at a hamburger joint?

Ending a Relationship becomes such an obsession that about the only time she cannot think about it is when she is golfing. It is, after all, a lot easier to break up a Relationship than it is to break ninety.

Breaking ninety requires more than rehearsal and reassurances. To break ninety you need skill, luck, and an expensive set of clubs.

A woman may not be able to break ninety because her wedge is jinxed, a bunch of branches keeps getting in her way, a water hazard is misplaced, or the foursome behind her is noisy. (Environment is more important to golf than it is to social interactions.) Missing a pitch in golf is not like missing a pitch in a conversation. A woman can't, after all, just try, try again in golf, as she can in an argument, and still hope to score well.

If a Relationship is going badly, your friends are there for you. Even your best friends, however, will not share your deepest divots in golf. Out on the course, if you play lousy, you play by yourself. No one wants to hear about it. You might affect their game. Likewise, if you break ninety, you break it yourself. Oh, a few friends may cheer you on. "That shot was great!" or "Make it a birdie!" Unlike in romance, though, in golf the game is yours alone to play; your best companions will offer as little advice as possible.

If you don't believe this, then meet your best golfing pal for dinner some night and see how long she will listen to your gut-wrenching stories of how poorly you are playing. "I just can't master the short game," you complain. "Why, I shot over 100 today! Four-putted every hole! I just can't play in my company tournament like this."

"Don't worry about it; it's just a game," she responds casually. "You can always take some lessons. Hey, not to change the subject, but I have to talk to you about something…something really important. It's about a Relationship!"

Cart-Mate Management

I have never met a woman golfer who did not outdrive a man. Think about the last time you golfed with a man. What did you spend your day doing? Were you chasing after your balls? Were you chasing after his balls? More likely, were you chasing after your golf cart? Women always drive better than men.

On a "Drive Wherever You Want" Course

Do you remember what happened the last time you went golfing with your significant other on one of those courses that let you drive wherever you want to go? To a man, golf-cart management means he will drive the cart halfway between your ball and his. He then will drop you off and head over to his. Always interested in your fast play, he won't bother giving you time to grab an extra club or two when he drops you off. "Take a 5-iron," he'll yell as he slows down so you can jump out.

So what if your ball is 200 yards from the green? You can hit it twice—once really hard and once really soft. Hey, maybe that way your next shot will be close to his, and you won't have to run very far to catch up with him. Considerate guy, huh?

On a Cart-Path-Only Course

Playing together on a course where you can drive wherever you want seems unpleasant until you remember what it was like sharing a cart with him on a cart-path-only course. Cart-path-only golf courses are owned by the smartest clubs around. This kind of club provides members the opportunity to get even more exercise than they would if they actually walked the course, but the club still is able to charge a cart-rental fee.

When you are riding with a man on a cart-path-only course, you will be treated much differently than you are when you are playing on a course with tire tracks. In fact, in this situation you usually will get to drive.

"What the heck, I don't want to be a chauvinist," he'll say. "Go ahead and take the wheel." You thus get the exclusive pleasure of running back and forth between ball and path every 150 yards or so.

Inevitably, on every hole, at whatever point you get out of your cart and get ready to head over to your ball, which may be 100 yards from his, he will yell out to you. "Since you are coming out this way, would you mind bringing me my 3-wood, 5-iron, pitching wedge, and putter?" He continues before you answer, "I'll tell you what. You go ahead and keep the cart. I'll meet you up at the green."

If more men would complain about clubs designating their courses as cart-path-only, the clubs would be forced to change. Men don't mind playing cart-path-only courses, though, especially if they are paired up with a caddie—I mean, a woman.

On a Ninety-Degree-Only Course

Most golfers play on courses that follow the ninety-degree rule. The ninety-degree rule, of course, is a rule that lets golfers drive anywhere they want on the course, provided it is at a right angle to the golf-cart path. I guess the theory is that that way all tire tracks will disadvantage all players equally.

Most men do not have a good understanding of the ninety-degree rule. They think it applies to their balls instead of their carts. These men thus pull out their drivers and slice and dice their way down the fairway. They think the ideal ball flight is perpendicular to their stance.

Women also fail to grasp the true intent of this golf-cart practice. A woman playing with a man acts as if the ninety-degree rule means that she should jump from the cart and hit the ground running while the cart is moving on a trajectory perpendicular to the green. To achieve this dramatic breakaway, the average woman leaves one foot dangling out of the cart at all times. Women have gotten hurt doing this. They have broken feet. They have broken ankles. They have broken kneecaps. They have broken almost everything except the average man's habit of slowing, rather than stopping, the cart when a woman needs to get out.

On Courses Where You Can Walk

Walking courses are a woman's best friend. Sure, it is unfortunate that a lot of courses that let you walk do not let you use a pull cart. Who cares, though? Walking courses are wonderful. When you golf and walk with the man you love, you really get a lot more enjoyment out of your game and each other. That darn golf cart is out of the way. You have absolutely nothing left to argue about.

There may, however, be one issue left for you to resolve. When men and women walk and golf, do women golfers still outdrive men? I think so.

Nineteenth Hole

After the Red Tees

Counting Scores, Settling Bets, and Buying Beers

People say golf is a game of concentration. They say it is a mental game. When you watch the pros on television you can see the mind-over-matter principle in action. A pro will stand over her ball and visualize it on the green. Bang! There it is.

Pros are not the only golfers who channel all their mental reserves through a single stick in motion, however. Even more than pros, amateur golfers—golfers like us—do so. In fact, among all the places where the game is played, and among all the people who play it, there is probably no better concentration to be found than that exerted by women golfers when we put pencil to paper and add up our golf scores.

There could be an earthquake, a riot, and a grass fire happening all at once (even on a golf course not in California) and women golfers adding up their scores would not even notice. Now that is concentration.

Most women, of course, tally their scores at the conclusion of play. Invariably, golfers who play well also believe they add well. "Wow! Can you believe I broke ninety?" asks a happy golfer with a 23 handicap who spent all of fifteen seconds adding up her score.

"That's great," responds the golfer who has tallied up her score three times, each time getting the same five-over-her-handicap score. "For some reason, I'm having trouble adding up my score. Could you do it for me?"

Some golfers keep track of their hooks and slices as they make them. For these golfers, the eighteenth hole is usually a sobering time, more of a letdown than a countdown. "If I had only birdied this number-one-handicapped par-5 hole, I could have broken 120."

Apart from match play, generally only poor golfers keep track of their score or of who is winning during a game. I suppose even poor golfers want to look good at something. They can't look good at their swings. The only viable way they have of looking good is being able to make themselves look bad sooner than anyone else can. Whether you count scores along the way or at the end, however, there is one pressing matter that must be determined before you put down your scorecards and go to the nineteenth: Who's buying?

Most women gamble for lunch or a round of drinks. No woman minds losing that kind of gamble. After all, the stakes are small and the steaks are smaller. It's worth it to celebrate someone else's victory. Women are never jealous of another golfer's success. We recognize that all women golfers are winners. Some of us just win a little more often than others.

Handicap Politics—Turning in the Scorecard

Some women golfers never, ever cheat during the game. They would be just as likely to take a mulligan or forgive themselves a whiff or a penalty shot as the average man golfer would be inclined to ask at the pro shop if he can be matched up with a female, rather than a male, threesome. Although some women golfers will not cheat *during* the game, all golfers, including women, will cheat *after* it.

According to the rules of golf, a golfer must turn in her score on every eighteen-hole game she plays. In reality, golfers, as a group, are very selective about what cards they turn in. There is, after all, no more difficult ethical or strategic question facing any golfer.

Oh, sure, there are a lot of tough decisions in golf. Should you lay up or go for it? Should you chip or putt? Should you count your last shot even though your opponent shouted right in the middle of it and that is the one and only reason you chili dipped? Should you use a driver or a club with which you can actually hit?

What is common to these questions, however, is that you will have only the outcome of one shot with which to contend after you decide how to proceed. The submission of a scorecard, on the other hand, does more than define your score on a single hole or even on all of the holes. Scorecards define your identity as a golfer.

Golfers do not suffer the identity crises other people do. They do not meditate with crossed legs and crosser attitudes, pondering "Who am I?" Name, rank, and handicap number—that is what a golfer's identity is made of.

High Handicappers

"Hi, I'm Sherri. I play from the red tees. I have a 32 handicap."

"Great, Sherri," says the pro who is signing golfers up for the tournament. "I'll put you in the high-handicap section. As soon as the championship, intermediate, and other real golfers tee off, you can head out with the other gals in your division."

Few high handicappers will feel indignant about this. The caste system in golf is not unconquerable. You can change your handicap and change your competition. Furthermore, all high handicappers know it is some cruel joke by the golf gods that they have been assigned to this caste anyway. They really play much better than their handicaps reflect. Their colleagues may hit poor shots and poorer putts, but their own handicaps are based on mischievous tree trunks and bad bounces.

Every high handicapper has the same dream: If only she could play five to ten games that accurately reflected her game. Then her handicap would decrease and would be an accurate indicator of her skill level. Until then, she has no choice, though. She must compete against the duffers. Those duffers keep making her duff up her game, too. As long as they do that, she will have to keep throwing away those horrible double- and triple-bogey finishes which luck throws in her way.

Her friend agrees. "That 128 just does not reflect how *well* you played today! I don't think you should turn your scorecard in. It just would not be fair to the other golfers."

"Well, okay," she agrees. "If you don't turn in your 137."

Neither one of them, after all, wants to remain in high-handicapper hell all of their golfing lives. A high handicap is more than an assignment to the hacker squad. It means you get no respect. Other golfers do not take high handicappers seriously. Furthermore, it is against proper golf etiquette for high handicappers to take themselves seriously.

Mid- and low-handicapped golfers do not want to play with a bunch of hackers. They think high handicappers play slow. Even other high handicappers would rather play with better golfers. Who wants to play against a 36+ handicapper and take a chance of losing gross?

You can always tell a high handicapper who is having a bad day or a low handicapper who is having a good one. They are the first ones in the nineteenth hole. Everyone else stopped by the pro shop to turn in their scorecards.

Low Handicappers

Low handicappers do not turn in their best scorecards, because they want their handicaps to go up. Of course, it takes years of practice and perfectionism to become a low handicapper. These players are not about to blow their games just to get some downright hideous double bogey. They will, instead, try to play their best; then, when they happen to play their worst, they will turn in their cards.

Other golfers do not understand what motivates low handicappers to do this. After all, there are more important things in life than winning a golf game. What about integrity? What about sportswomanship? Better yet, what about the absolute awe both men and women offer a woman who casually mentions she has a 5 handicap? Why would anyone give up single-digit stardom to join double-digit mediocrity?

The answer, of course, is that a golfer does not give up her bragging rights to the handicap she can count on one hand even after it has increased to include both hands and both feet. Unless you are setting up a bet, if you ask a low handicapper for her index, she will tell you what it is. Then (if it used to be better) she will tell you what it was.

Average Golfers

Average golfers are the golfers who are most apt to turn in their scorecards on a consistent basis. After all, average golfers generally don't have twenty-five-stroke spreads in their games and a three or four stroke spread does not make much of a percentage difference.

All average golfers want to lower their handicaps. They have too much integrity to play scorecard bingo with the pro shop, however. It just would not be fair. Average golfers thus turn all of their scorecards in—the good, the bad, and even the fraudulent.

The Ball That Got Away (and Other Recaps)

The average male golfer spends his time at the nineteenth hole figuring out who owes what to whom. His idea of small talk is a Nassau that is only five dollars. A man golfer is about as motivated in the nineteenth hole to talk about how he can improve his game as he is to tell the woman he loves just how much money he actually lost playing golf this year.

Since the average woman golfer, on the other hand, bets smaller and simpler (and, let's face it, smarter), she can take the time to talk about her game after she finishes playing it. In fact, women golfers are a little like fisherwomen. They recap and relive the biggest and best of their efforts and retool the rest to look like achievements.

Women Who Have Lost Balls

Consider the woman golfer who has lost a ball. She regards this the same way a fisherwoman would think of lost bait. No one fishing ever loses her bait to a minnow. It is always some record-busting bass that steals it away. Likewise, women golfers recognize that their lost balls accompanied their greatest shots. Mediocre shots land on fairways and greens. The great shots, however, are the ones whose magnificent soars are abruptly and unfairly halted by murky fishponds, misplaced shrubs, and muddy trenches. You find these women hard to believe? Then just ask the average man golfer. He'll tell you where his best shots go.

This, of course, is why so many men spend so much time looking for their lost balls on the course. Out on the twelfth hole, however, the woman golfer waves her friends away from the ravine where her ball headed. "That's okay, don't worry about it," she reassures them. "I have plenty of balls." What she does not tell them, however, is that though she is not taking five minutes out of everyone's time on the course to look for that little traitor, she does intend to hold a five-minute service today at the nineteenth hole for every ball she has lost.

The nineteenth hole, in fact, is the woman's requiem for "would have" "could have" "should have" scores that slipped away as gently and quietly as their owner's seventy-mile-per-hour swings. How and where one loses a ball is recycled for replay between bites of lunch. At the nineteenth hole, women golfers exchange stories of the lost ball that otherwise would have mattered. The ball would have made the difference between an 88 and a 90; a 98 and a 100; or a good day and a bad day.

Women Who Have Lost Aces

Women who want to talk about their lost balls have some stiff competition, however. There are other women golfers present who instead want to discuss the hole in one they just missed. Runaway-ace stories are like the fish-that-got-away stories. Usually a golfer with a "just missed" hole in one does not even birdie the hole. Her ball may have missed the hole by only a half-inch. It was, however, airborne at the time. It landed twenty feet past the hole and ended up in the frog hair on the back of the green. Of course, the golfer telling you the story is about as likely to tell you that as the starter is likely to tell you he has to move your tee time up a half hour earlier this Saturday because everyone has been playing so fast. Yet it's fun to listen to her tell the story. It certainly has a lot more appeal than listening to the men talk about their bets or that other woman golfer complaining about her three putts.

Women Who Three-Putt

Three-putters like to talk at the nineteenth hole about how poorly they putt. They want everyone listening to them to reach the same conclusion. "She's really not a bad golfer. She is just a lousy putter." It is, after all, much more preferable to have a lousy putt than a lousy game. Three-putters get tiresome after a while, though. Women enjoy hearing about other women's successes more than the reasons why they have none.

There is only one thing worse than listening to someone complain about how poorly he or she putted. That is listening to a golfer talk about how well—how very, very well—that golfer played. Since women golfers do not brag, that, of course, involves listening to a man.

From the sound of this, you would think women would avoid the nineteenth hole, yet all women golfers flock there after play. Obviously there is more to the nineteenth hole than recall and recap. A very important matter is discussed. Hang out there long enough and sooner or later the issue will be raised.

"Hey, when can we get together to play again?"

I hope the answer is soon—very, very soon. I'll be looking for you, too...on the red tees.

Lexicon

ace   An ace is a hole in one. To score an ace, you must be lucky, a pro, or lying.

alternate ball   A golf game in which members of a golfing team, usually composed of two golfers, take turns hitting one ball down the course. Often the rules are modified so that both golfers hit a tee shot on each hole; once the best tee shot is selected, the golfer whose tee shot was not used hits the second shot from where the best ball lies, and then the players continue alternating shots until that ball is in the hole. This format continues either throughout the game or throughout the number of holes for which it is the designated format. Alternate ball is often used as one of several formats in an eighteen-hole couples' tournament. The tournament may, for instance, employ the alternate-ball format for six holes, a two-person scramble for six holes, and best ball for six holes.

best ball   A team game in which each golfer plays her own ball on a hole but then uses the best (the lowest) score for the team score. In golfer parlance, however, sometimes a scramble is referred to as best ball.

birdie   A birdie is a score of 1-under-par. To birdie a par-4 hole is to

215

get the ball into the hole in only three hits. Birdies are wonderful scores to make.

bogey   A bogey is a score of 1-over-par. To bogey a par-4 hole is to get the ball into the hole in five hits. A bogey is a decent score for the average golfer.

carry   The distance between where a golfer hits a ball and where the ball lands. A golfer may hit a ball 175 yards, for instance, 160 yards of which is carry and 15 yards of which is roll. Carry is an important consideration when determining club selection for a shot over a water hazard or ravine.

chili dip   To chili dip a shot means to take an unsuccessful swipe at the ball whereby the ball goes only a very short distance. Usually a golfer chili dips her shot when she is close to the green and mistakenly looks up while swinging to see if her ball is going to make it onto the green. The term results from the arc resembling that of a cracker on its way into a chili dip. There is a substantial difference between the two kinds of dip, however. The golfer may like to eat chili dip, but she will not like to chili dip.

duffer   A golfer who does not play very well. Many golfers will humbly refer to themselves as duffers and will refer to golfers who play exceptionally well as "players."

eagle   An eagle is a score of 2-under-par. To eagle a par-4 hole is to get the ball into the hole in two hits. The average golfer expects to score an eagle as often as she expects to hit an actual eagle in flight.

five   A score of 5 on a hole indicates a golfer hit (or attempted to hit) her ball five times before it dropped into the hole.

Fore!   The universal shout of warning when a ball in flight looks as if it might hit people on the course. Duck for cover when you hear "Fore!" and shout "Fore!" when you see a ball heading for heads (or any other body parts).

flight   The trajectory of the ball.

gimme   The practice whereby a golfer picks up his or her golf ball when it is on the green and records a score that assumes the golfer would have putted the ball into the hole with one stroke. A golfer is most likely to take a gimme when her ball's distance from the hole is less than the length from the top of the leather to the clubhead on her putter. Thus arose the slang term "in the leather" for taking a gimme—and the demand for long putters.

golf ball   Golf balls come in various colors, weights, and brands. The United States Golf Association (USGA) has standardized golf balls so that the maximum permissible weight of a ball is 1.62 ounces, the maximum permissible diameter is 1.68 inches, and the maximum initial velocity must be no more than about 174 miles per hour.

Golfers generally play with balls that are white, but white balls with various logos are also common. Yellow, orange, and pink balls are seen infrequently on the golf course. I also have seen light blue balls, in a lady's brand, for sale in a pro shop.

There are too many brands of balls to mention. Some of the ones I refer to in this book are Titleist, Flying Lady, and Pinnacle. While they are all great balls, and there are other good brands, too, my current favorite, just in case anyone reading this is shopping for my birthday present, is Top Flite XL-W. (Do you think I should have called Top Flite to see if they would have paid me to say this?)

handicap   A system that adjusts a golfer's scores so that golfers of different abilities can engage in truly competitive play in which the winner cannot be assured at the outset. Generally, a handicap reflects how much under or over par a golfer played the best ten of her last twenty games. Golfers usually only shoot to their handicap if they are having a good day. A golfer with a 26 handicap is statistically more likely to shoot a 99 to a 101 on a par-72 course than the 98 her handicap suggests. The level of the difficulty of a course is controlled for when a pro shop assigns a golfer a handicap index.

hook   A golf swing that results in the ball going to the left. Better golfers usually have hooks.

in the zone   A golfer who is "in the zone" is focused and is playing her game better than usual.

lay up   To hit your ball so that it lands short of a water or sand hazard.

mulligan   To take a mulligan is to hit another ball with the understanding that you will not use your first ball or count that stroke in your score. While the USGA rules do not anticipate the use of mulligans, it is not unusual for golfers to allow themselves a mulligan (or even two) when playing eighteen holes.

Nassau   A three-part bet in which golfers wager on which team or player will win the front nine holes, the back nine holes, and the full eighteen holes.

par   To par a hole is to hit the same number of strokes on that hole that the course assigned to it on the scorecard. Thus, to par a par-four hole, you must hit the ball into the hole in four strokes. Most eighteen-hole courses have a par of seventy-two strokes.

pro-am A tournament that consists of professional and amateur golfers playing together. A best-ball format is not unusual.

scramble A golf game in which each team member tees off and then they pick the best ball to play. Each golfer then moves her ball to within a club length of that ball and hits again. The best ball is selected once again and each golfer moves her ball to hit from that location, and so on throughout the game. Scrambles are usually played in two-person or four-person teams.

scratch A golfer who has a zero handicap is commonly referred to as a scratch golfer. A scratch handicap is a zero handicap.

shank To shank a shot is to mishit the ball so that it is a bad shot. Shanked shots are often hit with the part of the club that connects the clubhead to the shaft, rather than hit with the clubface.

slice A slice is a shot that results in the ball curving dramatically to the right. Generally, good golfers have a tendency to hook, and average and not-so-good golfers have a tendency to slice. Both hooks and slices are caused by the spin motion of the ball. Clockwise spins result in slices and counterclockwise spins result in hooks.

takeaway The beginning part of a backswing.

tee The wood or plastic peg on which a golfer places her ball before hitting her first shot on a hole (which is why this first shot is sometimes referred to as her tee shot).

tee box The area on which the tees (the tee markers) are set. Most teeing grounds are at least slightly elevated, are box shaped, and are of sufficient size to easily accommodate a golfer taking a full golf swing (and often a couple of other golfers watching her from behind).

tees The area from which a golfer hits her tee shot. This area, or teeing ground, is identified on the course by tee markers. Traditionally, there are three sets of markers and they are respectively colored blue, white, and red.

The area designated by the blue tee markers, referred to as the *blue tees*, is the most challenging area from which a golfer may play a course, as the blue tees are the farthest distance from the hole. The *red tees*, often referred to as the "ladies tees," are the shortest distance from the hole. All women golfers, except when they are on an unusually short course or unless they are exceptionally strong golfers, play from the red tees. The *white tees* are located between the red and blue tees and are, or at least should be, the tees of choice for the average male golfer. A golfer plays from the same color tees throughout a game.

The proper teeing ground, or area to hit a tee shot from, is the area from the tees of choice to two club lengths back. It is against the rules of golf to hit a tee shot from a location in front of the tees from which one is playing.

three-putt To three-putt is to putt your ball three times before it goes into the hole. Pars on holes are generally set up so that the golfer will putt the ball twice. Thus a par-4 hole anticipates a scratch golfer will hit the ball twice to get on the green and putt the ball twice to get in the hole. If a golfer consistently takes three or more putts to get her ball in the hole, her score will be dramatically increased (worsened) by her poor putting.

topped ball A topped ball is a golf ball that is struck incorrectly; the golfer hits the top of the ball. Topped balls often become wormburners. "I topped it!" is one of the most common complaints of golfers after they hit a shot that results in a ball rolling rather than flying. A topped ball is often caused by a golfer coming up during her swing.

Vardon grip The overlapping golf grip. Harry Vardon, a famous golfer in the early twentieth century, used this grip; his name is commonly used to refer to it.

whiff To miss the ball while attempting to hit it. Whiffs differ from practice swings in that the golfer who whiffs a ball intended to hit it but missed. A whiff must be counted as a stroke; practice swings generally are not.

wormburner A wormburner is a ball that rolls quickly down the fairway after being struck by a golfer. Wormburners usually result from topped shots.

About the Author

Dorothy Langley is an insurance executive, an attorney, a Chartered Property Casualty Underwriter, and a slicer.

A graduate of Harvard Graduate School of Business Administration (M.B.A. 1989), the Washington University School of Law in St. Louis, Missouri (J.D. 1982), Boston University (B.A. 1979), and Massasoit Community College in Brockton, Massachusetts (A.A. 1977), Dorothy received her best business advice from her mother: "You had better learn golf if you want to get ahead, honey." Her father and several highly paid pros then taught her how to play the game.

Dorothy is a member of the Executive Women's Golf Association and several other leagues in the Dallas area. Dorothy's husband, Bryan O'Neill, occasionally golfs with her. However, he generally prefers piloting a plane over the course she is playing and buzzing her and the other members of her foursome.